Award-winning writer, television broadcaster and author of numerous bestsellers, **Leslie Kenton** is described in the press as 'the guru of health and fitness' and 'the most original voice in health'. A shining example of energy and commitment, she is highly respected for her thorough reporting. Leslie was born in California. She is the daughter of jazz musician Stan Kenton and Violet Peters, a painter. After leaving Stanford University she journeyed to Europe in her early twenties, settling first in Paris then in Britain where she has since remained. She has raised four children on her own by working as a television broadcaster, novelist, writer and teacher on health and for fourteen years she was an editor at *Harpers & Queen*.

Leslie's writing on mainstream health is internationally known and has appeared in *Vogue*, the *Sunday Times*, *Cosmopolitan* and the *Daily Mail*. She is the author of many other health books including: *The Joy of Beauty*, *Ultrahealth*, *Raw Energy* and *Raw Energy Recipes* – co-authored with her daughter Susannah – *Ageless Ageing*, *The Biogenic Diet*, *Cellulite Revolution*, *10 Day Clean-up Plan*, *Endless Energy*, *Nature's Child* and *Lean Revolution*. She turned to fiction with *Ludwig* – her first novel. Former consultant to a medical corporation in the USA and to the Open University's Centre of Continuing Education, Leslie has won several awards for her writing, including the PPA 'Technical Writer of the Year'. Her work was honoured by her being asked to deliver the McCarrison Lecture at the Royal Society of Medicine. In recent years she has become increasingly concerned not only with the process of enhancing individual health but also with re-establishing bonds with the earth as a part of helping to heal the planet. Leslie now lives in West Wales in an eighteenth-century house overlooking the sea, once inhabited by Virginia Woolf.

10 Day
De-stress Plan

Make stress work *for* you

Leslie Kenton

EBURY PRESS • LONDON

1 3 5 7 9 10 8 6 4 2

First published in the United Kingdom in 1994 by
Ebury Press
Random House
20 Vauxhall Bridge Road
London SWlV 2SA

Random House Australia (Pty) Limited
20 Alfred Street, Milsons Point, Sydney,
New South Wales 2061, Australia

Random House New Zealand Limited
18 Poland Road, Glenfield,
Auckland 10, New Zealand

Random House South Africa (Pty) Limited
PO Box 337, Bergvlei, South Africa

Random House Canada
1265 Aerowood Drive, Mississauga,
Ontario L4W 1B9, Canada

Random House UK Limited Reg. No 954009

A CIP catalogue record for this book is available
from the British Library.

ISBN 0 09 178420 4

Illustrator: Tony Hannaford

Typeset from author's disks by Clive Dorman & Co.

Printed and bound in Great Britain by Clays Limited, St Ives, plc.

Papers used by Ebury Press are natural recyclable products made
from wood grown in sustainable forests.

For Linda Griffiths

who has the courage to turn
uncertainty into challenge

Acknowledgements

I would like to give my special thanks to the following people for the help and inspiration they have given me over the years in my quest to find ways of using stress in the best way possible. To Hans Selye MD who, when we met in the Seventies, was a great inspiration to me. To Dr Peter Mansfield who shared with me his own profound understanding of the nature of wholeness. To Dr Andrew Strigner who taught me that the powers of the mind can be released through deep relaxation. To Dr Dagmar Leichti von Brasch and Dr Gordon Latto who taught me about de-stressing the body through nutrition. To Dr Philip Kilsby who first introduced me to the power of herbs. To Lama Zopa Rimpoche and Lama Thuben Yeshe who gave me patience to explore meditation at its depths. To Marilyn Mason who, after so many years of struggle, taught me to appreciate yoga, and Vera Diamond who first introduced me to autogenic training. To Graham Jones who taught me the way to transform my lounge lizard life into a highly active one, and to Julia Hastings for helping me understand the power of imagination. To Sarah Wallace for her enormous competence, patience and humour in editing not only this book but so many in past and hopefully even more in the future. And, finally, to my cat Carciofo who handles stress better than any creature I have met.

Leslie Kenton
Pembrokeshire 1994

Contents

DAY ONE
Aim High 9

DAY TWO
Clean Up 27

DAY THREE
Breathe Easy 43

DAY FOUR
Chill Out 66

DAY FIVE
Move Light 75

DAY SIX
Eat Well 90

DAY SEVEN
Get Clear 105

DAY EIGHT
Earth Works 116

DAY NINE
Sleep Deep 128

DAY TEN
Go Free 140

RESOURCES 153

INDEX 156

Day One

Aim High

We worry about stress, wonder about stress, and wish it would go away. Seldom do we stop to ask what it is. Little wonder. For stress is a complicated thing even to define. The word stress comes from the language of engineering, meaning 'any force which causes an object to change'. In engineering the specific change caused by stress is known as strain and there are four possible kinds – torsion, tensile, compression and sheering. In human terms the strain is your body's response to physical, chemical, emotional or spiritual forces, asking in some way that you *adapt* to them. The idea that stress is all bad is patent nonsense. Stress can be the spice of life, the exhilaration of challenge and excitement, the high of living with heavy demands on you. And, like the tempering process involved in the production of a piece of good steel, once you make a friend of stress, forces which once seemed to be working against you become positive energies that define you, strengthen you and help you express your own brand of creativity and joy. As Austrian-Canadian scientist, the late Hans Selye – often called the father of stress since he first coined the word in relation to humans back in the 1930s – used to say, 'Whatever does not destroy you only makes you stronger.'

This little book explores stress. It offers a compendium of techniques, information, practices and tools that can help you do two things: first, become more aware of how stress acts in your own life and, secondly, transmute a great deal of what you may be currently experiencing as negative stress into positive challenge. For the big secret about all kinds of stress is that what appears to be causing stress – the *stressor* – is seldom what causes damage. It is how you *respond* to what is happening that does that.

10 Day De-stress Plan is divided into ten days so that it can easily be read in no more than half an hour per day. It is designed to give you easy access to useful information and methods from which you can choose those that seem relevant to your life. If you are lucky enough to have a ten-day break, say on holiday, to explore in depth day by day what you find within, doing so will still not take up more than two hours of your day. If not, pick one or two areas, say a technique for deep relaxation or the clean-up diet to put into practice during the first week while you are reading the book. Then introduce another technique or method a week or fortnight later until gradually you discover for yourself what works best. What the *10 Day De-stress Plan* most adamantly does *not* ask is that you lay aside everything else in your life in order to do everything that you find within its pages. That in itself could be very stressful indeed! Each human being is unique. Some things will appeal to one person while to others they will have no attraction. It is a good idea to set aside half an hour to forty-five minutes a day for the reading and any notes you might like to do. However you decide to work with the book, aim high. For you are likely to be as surprised as I have been to discover that many of the best methods for turning negative stress to advantage can at the same time heighten your general wellbeing, enhance your sense of pleasure, increase your energy, and give you access to a more satisfying way of living. On Day One we look at the biochemistry of stress and the stress reaction. We also begin to explore how to make stress work *for* you rather than *against* you.

What is Stress?

Stress is hard to pin down: fatigue, overwork, loss of blood, physical damage, grief and joy can all produce stress, but not one of them accurately describes what it is. The leader of a mountaineering team faced with a difficult ascent on which the lives of his men depend is under stress. So is the woman who burns her hand cooking, and the child forced to walk home from school in the freezing rain. For although the conditions these people face are different and although each one's *specific* response varies – the mountaineer experiences sweating and tightness in the stomach, the woman shock and inflammation of her hand, the child shivering and pallor – they all respond in a stereotyped manner and undergo identical biochemical changes to help them cope with the increased demand on their organism. They all experience the same increased production of corticoid hormones and of adrenalin from the adrenal glands, for instance, as well as a number of other nervous, biochemical and physical shifts which together make up the stress response. And this is what human stress is all about. Selye has defined stress as 'the *nonspecific* response' of the body to any demand made upon it.

It is an important idea to grasp on the road to becoming stress-wise – that is in learning to make a friend of stress and making it work for you rather than against you. It is a difficult concept, too. For it seems funny to think that the body can respond to experiences as different as cutting

11

your hand and hearing the news that you have just won the Irish Sweepstakes in exactly the same manner.

A major key to handling stress is the realization that it is not the external stressors that make you suffer their negative effect. It is the way you *respond* to them. Change your response and you can turn negative into positive. This has been demonstrated again and again in objective quantitative research. The implications of these findings are simple: if one can meet stress as a challenge and if you can also eliminate as many unnecessary stressors as possible from your life, you can not only make a positive experience of stress but also protect the long-term health of your body, and have a lot of fun in the process. It is a tremendously exciting possibility. It means that we are not doomed to inevitable illness later in life, nor to the premature ageing we see happening around us. To quote the *Journal of the American Medical Association*: 'Nature did not intend us to grow old and ill; we were designed to die young in old age, but free of disease.' I would add to that, each of us is also designed to live out our unique creative energy in our own way. Stress well handled actually helps us to do this. More about how in later chapters. For now let's take a look at what happens to your body when you face any kind of stressor.

The Stress Reaction

The stereotyped biological stress reaction which Selye discovered and other scientists have confirmed is known as the *General Adaptation Syndrome* or GAS. The purpose of GAS is to maintain the structure and function of your body in a steady state know as homeostasis, and by doing so to preserve your life. Every 'stressor' with which you come into contact threatens to some degree to destroy homeostasis. The moment this happens the General

Adaptation Syndrome comes into operation. GAS has three recognizable stages: an initial *alarm* stage of alerting reaction; a stage of active *resistance*; and a stage of *exhaustion*. During the alarm reaction, as GAS is first set in motion, your overall resistance is lowered, the sympathetic nervous system fires, brain waves change, muscles tense, peripheral circulation increases and the adrenals secrete hormones more rapidly. During resistance it is all systems go as you are stimulated into increased activity in order to meet the challenge and protect you from harm – in effect your resistance is raised. This stage can last for a short or long while depending on your individual make-up, your attitude to the circumstances, and on the intensity of your reaction to the stressor. But it cannot go on forever. If stress remains, sooner or later the third stage of GAS is reached – exhaustion. Then organic illness becomes evident as the body's weakest systems begin to break down and chronic fatigue sets in. If this exhaustion stage continues, the body eventually dies.

You are Unique

Every individual differs in his reaction to stressors – a stressor to one person can be a source of exhilaration to another – although certain stressors, such as burning, affect everyone. People also vary widely in terms of how much stress they can take before reaching the exhaustion stage. This depends to some degree on your conditioning and on the amount of adaptive energy you were born with. Researchers still do not precisely understand adaptive energy, but they know it is not the same as caloric energy, which can be replaced by food. One person will have a great deal of adaptive energy – he may be on the move constantly and may be able to withstand a great deal of stress, while another, when faced with the same stress, quickly reaches the GAS exhaustion stage. As Selye used to say, 'If you are a racehorse you have to be a race-horse but if you are a turtle and you try to behave like a racehorse you are asking for trouble.'

Selye believed that once adaptive energy is used up, as a result of the wear and tear of stress, nothing could be done to restore it. We now know this is not altogether true (see Day Eight), but adaptive energy is certainly precious. This makes it imperative to examine carefully how yours is being used and if it is being burnt up un-necessarily. It also makes it important to remember that *what goes up must come down*. These few words should be engraved on the brain of every Western man and woman – particularly those of us who opt for a high-energy lifestyle. For experiencing high energy in a healthy way – not by taking drugs, drinking coffee or burning your-self out – depends on your being able to switch off at will. This is something that most of us have to *learn* to do. After all, urban civilized life is not the best possible en-vironment for keeping you in touch with life's natural rhythms. Yet acknowledging these rhythms – from alter-ations in light and darkness to the way in which outflow-ing energy needs to be balanced by restorative inflowing energy – is central to maintaining a high-level vitality and to gaining stress-wisdom. Stress (or the high-energy lifestyle) and relaxation are like two sides of a coin. Learn to move easily from one to another and you will begin to experience your life as a satisfying and enrich-ing challenge like the ebb and flow of the tides. Then you will never again have to worry about getting stuck in a high-stressed condition which saps your vitality, distorts your perceptions and can even lead to premature ageing and chronic illness.

Fight or Flight

Human beings are natural seekers of challenge. In prim-
itive times the challenge was one of survival, and this
gave a certain rhythm to the working of the body. When
in danger from some external cause – say, a wild animal
– the body reacted instantaneously, providing the energy
resources to fight or flee. The physiological changes
brought about in the body by stressors are described as
the *fight or flight mechanism.* Adrenal secretions flash into
the blood and bring strength in the form of fat and sugar
energy to the brain and muscles. The pulse races, blood
pressure increases and breathing speeds up. Within
seconds the body's full energy potential is realized, so one
can deal effectively with the threat – either by fighting and
destroying it or by running away to safety. Both actions use
up all the chemical by-products of the stress reaction – the
sugar, the adrenalin – and the increased muscle strength
that accompanies them. When the danger passes, the
body relaxes. The production of adrenalin slows to a
trickle and heartbeat and breathing decrease. The body
returns to its vegetative rhythm, restoring normality to
physiological processes and bringing a sense of mental
and physical wellbeing.

We are biologically the same creatures as those a
million years ago who fought or fled from wild animals.
Our bodies still react to danger in the same way, but
now our sense of danger comes from different threats –
the pressure of deadlines at work, the fear that someone is trying to take your job from you, or worry about
losing the closeness of the person you love most if you do
what *you* really want to do instead of what he or she wants
you to do. All these and many other reasons cause someone to move into the danger rhythm state without suffering physical or mental damage. The trouble is that

modern life, with its noise, quick pace, social pressures, environmental poisons, and our orientation to sedentary mental work, presents many of us with almost constant threat situations. This is particularly true in the business world where someone, instead of moving rhythmically out of the danger state into the vegetative one, remains for long periods (in some cases every waking hour) in the danger state with all the internal physical conditions that accompany it. Then blood pressure rarely goes down to normal, pulse remains rapid, and muscles and brain are activated by the production of adrenalin but have no physical outlets for this increased energy. Sooner or later, unless they move out of the threatening situation, the predator who at one time preyed on the wild beast, begins to prey internally on him or herself.

Getting the Balance Right

The automatic or involuntary functions of your body are governed by the autonomic nervous system. It looks after the changes in the rate at which your heart beats. It regulates your blood pressure by altering the size of veins and arteries. It stimulates the flow of digestive juices and brings on muscular contractions in the digestive system to deal with the foods you take in. It makes you sweat when you are hot and is responsible for the physical changes in your body that come with sexual arousal. This autonomic system has two opposing branches: the *sympathetic* and the *parasympathetic*.

The sympathetic branch is composed of a group of nerve fibres radiating from the spinal cord and linked with the catecholamines – the adrenalin class of hormones. It is concerned with expansiveness and energy expenditure, particularly the energy involved with stress and meeting challenges. It spurs the heart to beat faster, makes you breathe hard, encourages you to sweat, and raises your blood pressure. It also inhibits the secretion of gastric juices and digestion and sends blood to the muscles to get you ready for action. The other branch of the autonomic nervous system – the parasympathetic – is made up mostly of nerve fibres from the vagus or tenth cranial nerve. Its activity is linked with the acetylcholine class of hormones. This branch is concerned with rest and regeneration rather than action. The workings of the parasympathetic branch are more or less in opposition to those of the sympathetic branch. The parasympathetic branch slows your heartbeat, reduces the flow of air to your lungs, stimulates the digestive system and helps relax your muscles.

When you are in a state of stress, the sympathetic nervous system has precedence over the parasympathetic. When you are relaxed, the parasympathetic branch is dominant. A good balance between the two is the key to stress-wise living as well as a door to enormous energy and continuing health. Balance makes it possible for you to go out into the world to do, to make, to create, to fight, and to express yourself as well as to retire into yourself for regeneration, rest, recuperation, enjoyment, and the space to discover new ideas and plant the seeds of future actions. Unfortunately, few of us get the balance right by accident. We have to learn.

Instead there is either the dynamic person who is always seeking greater challenges and heights of personal achievement and who seems to have endless energy – until she discovers a few years on that she is suffering from high blood pressure and is told either to ease up or to go into long-term drug therapy for hypertension. Or, at the other extreme, the gentle, quiet, sensitive person who luxuriates in physical comforts, dreams beautiful dreams, and impresses everyone with her serenity, but who never seems able to put any of her ideas into effective action. The first person is what is known as a *sympathetic-dominated* person. The second is called *parasympathetic-dominated*. To make the most of your potential in the world and still remain well enough and receptive enough to enjoy the fruits of your labours, you want to be neither – or both.

Two Sides of a Coin

Under stress your body consumes more oxygen, its metabolic rate increases, your arteries contract, the concentration of lactates in your blood goes up, and your heart beats faster. During stress, cortisone levels in the body are increased. Over a long period this tends to block out the immune response – one of the main reasons why you become less resistant to disease when you are under constant stress. All these changes are reversed when you go into a state of psychophysical relaxation: cardiac rate decreases, lactate levels fall, there is a decrease in oxygen consumption, and your body returns to a regenerative state.

The secret of getting the right balance between stress and relaxation, between the sympathetic and the parasympathetic branches, is threefold, First, take a look at the kind of stress that is part of your life, eliminate unnecessary stressors and discover new ways of working with the others. Secondly, learn one or more techniques for conscious relaxation and practise them until they become second nature. Finally, explore ways for expanding your mind, honouring your individuality and for creating an environment that supports both. Not only will this help your body stay in balance and increase your level of overall vitality, it can bring you a sense of control over your life that is hard to come by any other way.

Making Stress Work for You

Begin by taking a look at how you may be wasting your adaptive energy by putting yourself under *unnecessary* stress. Try to identify unnecessary stressors in your life. By eliminating as many as you can you free a lot of energy for more positive use. For instance, physical inactivity is a stressor – it decreases your body's ability to function at optimum levels, it encourages the storage of wastes in the muscles and skin, and makes you chronically fatigued. So instead of indulging in it, start some kind of exercise programme – swimming or running or dancing – and follow it regularly three or more times a week (Day Five). It is now medically established that the better shape you are in, the easier you will find it to handle stress. Taking the time to participate in some physical activity also reflects a particular psychological attitude to yourself and your body – an attitude which will lead you to react in new, more positive ways in your work, your relationships with people, and your personal values. Many people who take up regular exercise report that they experience conceptual shifts so that things which appeared stressful before no longer bother them. That annoying woman on the bus every morning who raises your blood pressure by humming the same tune under her breath suddenly no longer bothers you. She becomes an object of pity or amusement and no longer one of your stressors.

Like cigarettes and drugs, various foods and drinks can be heavy stressors, too. They offer nothing in the way of positive health and vitality, but are a constant drain on the adaptive energy in your body. It is well established that caffeine, alcohol, tobacco, sugar and excess fat are stressors. They are substances your body not only doesn't need but which actively work against its normal healthy functioning. Become aware of this (Day Six) and decide to eliminate some of them from your life. In three months' time you won't miss them.

Many emotional stressors can also be discarded. Take a look at what continues to trigger off the stress response in your life and ask yourself whether you really want to meet this challenge – for instance a relationship which doesn't work or a job you hate – or whether it is something which prevents you from turning a lot of your creative energies to more constructive use. Some stressors provide challenges from which one can grow. Others are simply habitual. They lead nowhere and bring little in terms of increasing awareness or ability to make better use of life. You might like to start a journal in which you record observations and feelings about your own life. Take a look at the work you do and ask yourself if you find it really satisfying. Are the financial responsibilities you have taken on really necessary? Can you reduce them in any way? If not, you might just try having the courage to drop some of them and accept the changes this will bring about. We all have a tendency to hang on to the status quo at all costs. Usually the cost is heavy in terms of lost creativity and life. Even if you learn the world's finest techniques for meditation and stilling the mind, if you are in a job you hate year after year or are faced with a relationship that no longer has meaning for you, they will do little good. Each of us not only needs to face up to the demands of stress, but to take responsibility for removing it wherever it is no longer useful and relevant to us. Are you one of those miracle-working superhumans who works from 9 to 5 – or 6 o'clock or 7 o'clock – and then comes home to look after home and family and relatives and friends? Do you do the shopping and the errands, and the feeding of partner or children, and still expect yourself to emerge from it at the end of the day a scintillating wit? This is what I call playing the superhuman role – a role which is commonplace among creative and ambitious people – particularly women. It is a dangerous game to play. Push yourself to your limits and you could find that you produce physical symptoms like headaches, colds and 'flu, back or neck or shoulder ache, chronic fatigue and PMT, or emotional troubles – which could be anything from feelings of inadequacy to depression, irritability and dependence on alcohol or drugs. You could also find that you are not doing the best for your job or the people closest to you, even though you may actually have been sacrificing your own needs to theirs. Many an intimate relationship has failed as a result of the superhuman syndrome. Don't let it happen to you.

Write it Out

At this point I suggest you make a list of everything you think of as a stressor in your life – anything that causes you to feel stressed. Now make yourself a chart like the one on page 22 and write down each of your stressors in the left-hand column. Think carefully about each one and decide whether it is possible to drop that stressor altogether, to change it in some way, or to embrace it – to turn it from a negative object of fear into a challenge. For instance, if you have too many financial commitments, can any of them be eliminated? If your television is rented could you do without it and what would be the consequence? You might find that you suddenly have much more time for yourself. If your work is a stressor is there anything you can do to change it or, better still, embrace it as a challenge? If you are eating too much fat, sugar and white flour, decide to make an effort to alter your diet. At the end of these ten days take a look at your plan in the light of what you have learned and see if there are any further changes you would like to make.

STRESS TRANSFORMATION

Stressor	Drop	Change	Embrace	Consequence
I spend too much money	Do without the television			More time for reading and relaxation
I am always tired		Eat a stresswise diet or seek health advice		Feel stronger and healthier
I hate certain aspects of my work			Face each problem as a challenge to be enjoyed	More self-respect and enjoyment of work, and less worry about it outside the workplace

In the meantime take a look at these general guidelines and see if you can apply any of them day by day.

● **Stop doing everything yourself**
Start delegating both at work and at home and, whenever you can, get someone else to do what needs to be done.

● **Reach for the top but never struggle in vain**
Take a close look at your values. What really matters to you? You can't have everything. Make choices and rejoice in the freedom such choice-making will bring you. Otherwise you could end up a workhorse who is ultimately not very good at anything.

● **Don't say yes to everything**
When something is asked of you, give yourself time to consider the request before you immediately agree. Is it something you can handle with relative ease? What are you going to have to lay aside to do it? What is it going to cost you in terms of time? All these things need to be considered before you agree to any request either at work or at home.

● **Forget the hero image**
So many people assume that they are supposed to be able to do everything. You are not. You are only human. And you'd be surprised how much pleasure it can bring to other people when they feel they can do something for you for a change. Express your needs and many of them are likely to be satisfied. Lock them away behind the perfectly together superhuman image you project and you go it alone.

● **Guard your time jealously**
Limit the time you spend on inessential things such as

seeing people you don't really care about seeing just because you feel it is expected of you. Cut back on the chores you feel you have to do. Do you really have to? Or could somebody else do them for you? Or could they remain undone for the sake of your peace of mind?

● Sort your priorities

Take a look at what is absolutely essential to your life and what is marginal. If you can write these things down on a piece of paper, then make sure the time and effort you spend on each thing is in line with these priorities. Take an active role in deciding how you will spend your time and live your life. Don't just let it happen.

● Create a routine

From day to day you need to make sure you have time to relax and to take care of yourself and time to spend with the people you love. No partnership will flourish without time spent together. Recreation and having fun are as important as hard work, responsibility and success. Make sure you get the balance right.

● Wind down from work

Arriving home from a long day's work can be the lowest point in one's day. You get through the front door, sigh with relief and suddenly feel how overwrought you are. Adrenalin and things to do have kept you going all day, but now you're ready to collapse with nervous exhaustion. You may go straight to the refrigerator and begin to sample snack after snack – hoping that eventually you'll find the magic food to calm and restore you. Or you may collapse in front of the television set and watch a programme you hate but haven't got the energy to turn off. For parents the problems are compounded by walking into the house and immediately having others make

24

demands on you. Start by recognizing the signs of stress
such as muscle tension, or a voracious and insatiable
appetite. Then make a conscious effort to help yourself
de-stress. If you are hungry when you come in, have a
piece of fruit to tide you over until dinner. Don't just
eat whatever you can find. It is likely to be a poor combi-
nation of food groups which will put even more stress on
your body and exhaust you still further. Also, eating when
you are nervous will not help your digestion and you are
likely to feel bloated and headachy. Make use of the
helpful de-stressors and treat yourself to one each day
after work or whenever you need to calm yourself down
and let go.

● **Exercise at the end of the day**
Many people find that doing half an hour's aerobic exercise straight after work is just what they need to shake off
the work-time worries and give them a new burst of energy.

There is no question that some people handle stress
better than others. They are what psychologists call *stress-
hardy* people. Stress-hardy personalities have three characteristics. They like challenges. They embrace
commitment. They are in control of their lives. Stress-
hardies tend to look at potentially difficult events and situations as challenges rather than things to be feared. Even
working sixteen hours a day for three weeks to complete
a project can be challenging and exciting provided that
you've made a real commitment to the undertaking and
provided that commitment has genuine meaning for
you. Without commitment, such a project can be very
unrewarding as well as damaging.

Being in control really works when dealing with stress.
People who feel in control of a situation experience a
sense of empowerment. Those of us who feel unable to

affect our environment tend to feel helpless. Helplessness leads to anxiety and then to depression. Lack of control can also be very damaging to the body long-term. The next nine days are about helping you to explore and experience some of the tools, ideas, techniques and practices that can help build a stress-hardy personality. Few stress-hardy people are born. Most are made through facing the demands of stress and turning fear into challenge. It is like learning to play a new game – a game which is both a lot of fun and brings big rewards.

Day Two

Clean Up

The first step to using food as a means of enhancing your body's ability to handle stress is to detoxify your body. It is this principle that keeps the luxurious and expensive health farms and beauty spas all over the world earning money hand over fist. When you eliminate foreign substances from your blood, organs, glands and tissues – the prime purpose behind a detox – you begin to feel balanced and clear headed. The look of your skin improves too, your energy levels are increased and your body starts to return to a healthy homeostasis. It is as simple as that – no magic and no necessity to pay a fortune for it. In the process of re-balancing metabolism for stress-hardiness you need only dissolve the old and build anew.

Every minute 300,000,000 cells in your body wear out and need to be replaced. A spring-clean diet – even for a few days – is a great beginning. The second step to being stress-wise with food is equally important. To maintain the new feeling of wellbeing after your body has been internally cleansed, you might like to exchange some of your careless eating habits for new ones that provide your system with everything it needs for strength and balance, as well as very little of what it *doesn't* need. With the *10 Day De-stress Plan* you can experience this for yourself by carrying out a three-day detox to spring-clean your body, balance any excess acidity from high stress by alkalinizing your system, and setting the scene for Day Six when you can begin stress-wise eating as the basis of a whole new lifestyle.

Go Raw

The basis of the best clean-up diet is fresh raw food. Fresh foods grown in healthy soil and eaten raw have the highest concentration of vitamins and minerals in easily usable form of anything you can eat. Raw foods have remarkable properties which is why they form the core of regenerative and rejuvenating diets at the world's most exclusive spas and clinics from the Golden Door in California to the Bircher-Benner Clinic in Zürich. In such places people spend several thousands of pounds in order to emerge at the end of a week or a fortnight looking and feeling years younger, leaner and more energetic.

This is because a diet of mostly raw fruits and vegetables has the ability to spring-clean the body from the inside out. It helps dissolve and eliminate toxic materials and stored wastes which have formed in various parts of the body, clear out the digestive system, restore a good acid/alkaline balance to the cells and generally stimulate the proper functions of organs and tissues. It puts you through a kind of transformation that leaves you sparkling with vitality and feeling centred, rested and able to tackle high-energy demands with ease. Physicians and biochemists have found that raw-food diets have curative properties which no one has yet fully explained. A Swedish scientist has discovered that health-giving substances occur in raw foods which he believes may even be capable of enhancing the genes passed on from parents to children. Another researcher named these substances 'auxones' and insisted that the absence of them in a diet results in mesotrophy – 'half-nutrition' or 'half-health'.

The notion that a diet of raw food can significantly improve one's health and enhance your body's ability to deal with stress is not a new one. Ancient physicians used raw-food diets for healing as have some pioneers in twentieth-century medicine. American researcher Dr S. M. Pottenger in California experimented for several years with 900 cats. He put some on a diet of raw food, others on cooked food, and monitored their health and reproductive capacities from generation to generation. He discovered that, while those on raw food fared very well, those on cooked food suffered from degenerative illnesses such as bone abnormalities, teeth problems and malformation of the jaw. He also found that by changing the diets of those on cooked food and giving them raw food instead, plus cod liver oil, he could greatly improve their condition and reverse or retard the degeneration. Later he tried the same principles out on his human patients, treating a great many illnesses with a diet of raw fruit and vegetables and unpasteurized milk. He even went so far as to give his patients a raw liver 'cocktail' made in a blender and seasoned with fresh herbs. The mixture was revolting – according to many who have been treated at the Pottenger Clinic in Southern California – but the results were superb. People got well.

Swiss physician Max Bircher-Benner (famed for advocating the fruit muesli which still carries his name) found that raw food has an ability to prevent 'digestive leuco-cytosis' – an immune reaction which consists of the mobilization of white blood corpuscles that concentrate on the walls of the intestines when one eats a cooked meal.

Bircher-Benner claimed, and his claim has since been supported by others, that eating raw food leaves the white corpuscles free for other tasks, saving your body the effort of non-essential defensive action and helping to strengthen its overall resistance to disease.

Professor Eppinger at the University of Vienna discovered that fresh raw foods raise the micro-electrical potential of living cells. This, he claimed, stimulates cell metabolism and increases both the cell's resistance to damage and its reproductive powers. Eppinger also showed that the enzymes in raw food encourage the full assimilation of vitamins and minerals. Without them, the nutrients may be present in your diet but your body may be unable to make use of them – particularly if its own enzyme systems do not function as well as they should because of any form of stress or chronic illness.

Green Glorious Green

When you hear the word green, does it conjure up images of Friends of the Earth and rainforests? Then think again. Green sizzles with power not only to help clean up your body but to protect it in the future from the damage caused by a high-energy lifestyle. Many of the raw green foods – spirulina, chlorella, green barley, alfalfa and algae for instance – are wonderful detoxifiers. They, too, help cleanse the body at a deep level and eliminate toxic wastes such as heavy metals. Secondly, green foods are rich in minerals to help re-balance the body's metabolic processes – impaired as a result of our factory-farmed, processed foods which deplete us of the minerals and micro-nutrients on which our metabolic machinery depends.

Green foods are superfoods – so powerful in their life-supporting abilities that the Japanese, who lead the world in nature-based health products, pay premium prices for them. Fresh-water algae such as spirulina and chlorella as well as freeze-dried young green plants like alfalfa, wheat grass and barley are all carefully prepared to preserve the living properties of raw foods. The Japanese call them wonderfoods for they are packed with minerals, amino acids (which your system fairly soaks up the moment you swallow them) and – most important of all – enzymes, the very stuff of life itself. Scientists once believed that all enzymes were destroyed in the stomach when you ate raw foods. Now we know that this is not so – that many are taken through into the system to set your skin and body's energetic molecules in motion, helping to create clearer, fresher skin, more vitality and heightened resistance to stress. For, while the physical by-product of stress tends to be acid, green foods alkalinize your system. This restores balance and creates a feeling of being centred and calm during highly demanding times. Get to know some of the 'greens' and those you like the best use often.

Sparkling Spirulina

A near-microscopic form of blue-green fresh-water algae, spirulina is made up of translucent bubble-thin cells stacked end to end to form an incredibly beautiful deep green helix. Spirulina is one specific form of blue-green algae of which there are more than 25,000 varieties on the earth. Some three and a half billion years ago these algae began to fix nitrogen from the atmosphere and to convert it into carbon dioxide and sugars and in the process release free oxygen. In time this created the oxygen-rich atmosphere in which the rest of life was able to develop. The whole process took over one billion years to complete.

So prolifically does spirulina grow when properly culti-vated that an area only the size of Wales could feed 6 billion people – the estimated population of the planet by the year 2000. That is why spirulina is currently being investigated as at least part of the answer to protein and nutrient shortages in Third World countries. In Chad in Africa where it grows wild, it has been used for centuries as the major source of protein – eaten raw in the form of sun-dried patties which form naturally at the banks of the lakes in which it grows.

Spirulina is unique and remarkable in so many ways that it is hard to list them all but it is probably the single most important nutritional supplement you can use to support good metabolism in this age of pollution in which we live. The amino-acid balance in spirulina is unique – in its balance of one amino with another it is closest to that found in human breast milk. Not only is it higher in complete bio-available protein than any other known food, it offers amino acids in a superb balance and in a form of protein which is easier to digest than any other kind. It is also lower in fat than any other kind of protein. Finally, the protein in spirulina, unlike that in meat or fish, eggs or most vegetable foods, is *alkaline* in character rather than acid. This can be very important when you are in the process of detoxifying the body or using it to balance stress demand on the body since most of the stored wastes you want to get rid of are acid in nature.

Also contained within this extraordinary plant – a plant without leaves or roots, seeds, flowers or fruit, which grows by the hundred in a single drop of pure water – are some other important nutrients in highly bio-available form. Take vitamin B12 for instance – important in protecting you from anaemia. Spirulina is nature's richest wholefood source of this vitamin. It is two to six times richer than raw beef liver which is generally touted as ideal. The iron content of spirulina is also the best in nature. Spirulina has 58 times more iron than raw spinach and 28 times more than raw beef liver. It is also the richest wholefood source of vitamin E (three times richer than raw wheatgerm) and of beta-carotene (25 times richer than raw carrots), which is the precious anti-oxidant precursor to vitamin A so essential for building good skin and connective tissue. Spirulina is probably nature's richest wholefood source of anti-oxidant nutrients – essential in protecting your body against ageing and degeneration – since it contains just about every one known, including the vitamins C, B1, B5 and B6, the minerals zinc, manganese and copper, the sulphur-based amino acid methionine and the trace element selenium, in addition to beta-carotene and vitamin E.

Father of Foods

For many, many generations before they started eating it themselves the Arabs used alfalfa as feed for horses, knowing that it made the animals strong and fast. When they finally tried this grass on men they found so many benefits from eating it that they named it al-fal-fa which means father of all foods. Alfalfa contains eight enzymes which are known to promote beneficial chemical reactions enhancing the assimilation of foods that you eat. It is also rich in vitamins A, E, K and D, as well as the bioflavonoids and many of the B-complex vitamins including pantothenic acid (particularly important for stress), vitamin B12 and vitamin B6.

Alfalfa contains an abundance of alkaline minerals, especially calcium and iron, potassium and magnesium. The alfalfa seed is more than 40 per cent complete protein. Alfalfa also boasts oestrogen-like substances which many natural practitioners claim are very helpful in the treatment of some menopausal conditions and pre-menstrual tension in many women. You can either sprout alfalfa seeds or you can get dried essence of young alfalfa sprouts in powder form which you can make drinks out of or sprinkle onto soups and salads.

Green Wonder

Another green wonder is dried essence of young barley. It was developed by the Japanese as part of the search for a completely natural nutrient-rich food to supplement poor diets. Grown organically and bursting with life-giving nourishment, this brilliant green powder is also great on a spring-clean diet or when recovering from a bout of stress or illness. It is usually taken between meals in quantities of 2–8 tablets – or 1 teaspoon to 1 tablespoon of the powder in a glass of water – three times a day.

Living Green

The second important fresh-water algae is chlorella which has such amazing energy-producing abilities that it can reproduce itself every 24 hours. The substance in the chlorella plant which makes this growth possible is known as CGF (Chlorella Growth Factor). Chlorella gets its name from its high content of chlorophyll. It contains more chlorophyll than any other known plant as well as lots of vitamins, minerals, dietary fibre, nucleic acids, enzymes, amino acids and other beneficial substances. Chlorella has an ability to strengthen the immune system – an important property when enhancing your body's ability to deal with stress. It has even been shown to increase interferon levels. It is also very rich in DNA and RNA, both of which many experts in natural medicine believe help to protect against stress and premature ageing when taken in supplement form. The cell walls of this algae help eliminate heavy metals and poisonous hydrocarbons from the plant. This may be one of the reasons chlorella is considered such a good detoxifier in the human body. It is taken in similar amounts to green barley and comes either in tablet or in powder form. Be warned – they are pricey.

Scents of the Sea

Sea plants are a good way of re-mineralizing the body after having lived on a Western diet of processed foods for a long time. Take kombu for instance – the brown algae used as medicine in Japan against mental problems, high blood pressure, paralysis and for wound healing – or red algae rich in B-complex vitamins, and in agar-agar which is good for digestion, or the green algae which have anti-inflammatory properties. There are other sea plants, too, with anti-fungal, anti-viral and anti-bacterial properties. As a whole this group of plants has been shown to bind and remove toxic heavy metals from the body – even radio-active strontium. Most sea plants are ultra-rich in the naturally balanced minerals which are needed for all the body's metabolic processes to work in top form.

Get into Green

You can take the greens in powder form, either in juice or in a hot drink like vegetable broth, two or three times a day just as you might drink tea or coffee. You can also take them in capsules. The seaweeds you can soak and add to your salads, soups or vegetable dishes, or they, too, can be taken in the form of kelp in capsules or tablets. I find the best way is to drink a glass of green drink between meals or even as a meal replacement in the evenings when you don't feel hungry (see Resources). I carry some of these magic greens around with me when I am travelling and use them when I am on the move or am unable to get food of a quality that I would ordinarily eat at home. For some people they take a bit of getting used to. In time you may come to like them so much that you don't even bother to mix these green powders with fruit or vegetable juice but take them, as I do, stirred into spring water.

A high-raw food regimen plus greens for three days helps clear out your whole system mentally and physically and leaves you feeling clearer and more centred. It is a first step along the road to stress-wise eating. It is also a way to discover for yourself how much greater your potential for good looks, energy and emotional enthusiasm is than you probably believe. You can use such a clean-up diet in another way too: every few months you can always go back to it for a few days to revitalize yourself whenever you feel you need it, perhaps at the changing of the seasons – particularly at the end of the winter and at the beginning of the autumn. You can also spend beneficial weekends on this regimen whenever you have over-indulged – at holiday times, for instance. It will straighten you out faster than anything else I know. But there is only one way you can find out what raw food can do for you: try it.

Breakfast

Bircher Muesli.
or
Yoghurt Energy Blend plus a piece or two of fresh fruit or a glass of fresh fruit juice, if desired.

Mid-morning

A glass of green drink made with fresh vegetable juice, fruit juice or spring water.

Lunch

Appetizer – choose from a slice of melon, avocado vinai-grette or a bowl of clear consommé.

Large salad of raw vegetables.

A baked potato with low-fat cottage cheese or a small bowl of brown rice, or 1–2 slices of wholegrain bread/toast.

A piece of fresh fruit.

Lunch is designed in such a way that you can eat your spring-clean meal at a restaurant as easily as at home. Here are some suggestions for a packed lunch.

A large salad (undressed) in a Tupperware container.

Salad dressing taken separately (if you pre-dress your salad it will go soggy).

A hard-boiled egg or some nuts/seeds.

A slice or two of wholegrain crispbread.

A piece of fresh fruit.

Mid-afternoon

A glass of green drink made with fresh vegetable juice, fruit juice or spring water.

Dinner

Bircher Muesli.

A slice of toasted wholegrain bread with a little honey or sugarless fruit jam, such as those made by Whole Earth.

Drinks

On a high-raw diet you may not be thirsty because the foods themselves have not been dehydrated by cooking and are therefore rich with organic fluids. Don't drink water with your meals but drink 6 to 8 big glasses a day *between* meals. The spring-clean diet eliminates coffee, tea, soft drinks and alcohol. Drink fresh vegetable and fruit juices, spring water (carbonated or plain), vegetable broth and herb teas instead. The trick to making good cups of herb tea is first to find several herbs or herb combinations which you enjoy and then add one or several of the following:

- A squeeze of lemon juice or a slice of lemon.
- A teaspoon or so of lightly scented clear honey such as acacia or clover.
- A drop of skimmed milk (especially nice with spicy teas).
- A dash of cinnamon.
- Try making a strong pot of your favourite tea and adding a sliced peach to it. Sweeten with honey, then chill for a couple of hours and drink iced in tall glasses.

HERB TEAS	
Peppermint	For settling an upset stomach
Lemon Verbena or Lemon Grass	Good tonics
Camomile	Calms the nerves
Golden Rod (Solidago)	A diuretic for those who retain water
Lime Blossom or Passion Flower	Good for relaxation
Comfrey	Cleanses the body of toxins

If you have been a heavy coffee drinker you may experience a headache or even a bit of nausea as the caffeine is clearing from your system.

Coffee – the 'Pick-me-up Throw-me-down' drink

Coffee drinking leads to chronic fatigue. Caffeine, like concentrated sugar, is a heavy stressor. It stimulates the pancreas to produce more insulin. If you regularly drink a lot of coffee your pancreas can become 'trigger happy' so that too much insulin is produced, thus lowering the blood-sugar levels. This can result in hypoglycaemia and the chronic fatigue and high body stress that accompanies it, which, in a kind of vicious circle, leads to more coffee drinking. (See also page 93).

Vegetable Juice

The ideal replacement for coffee or tea, vegetable juice gives you a similar energy pick-up but without the subsequent let-down associated with caffeine. If you have your own centrifuge juice extractor it will make excellent vegetable and fruit juices. Combine carrot and apple in a ratio of 6:4 for a really delicious drink. Experiment with adding other vegetables such as cucumber, celery and spinach (but not potato) to a carrot base for an excellent vitamin and mineral-rich tonic. You can take fresh juice to work in a thermos flask with ice added. If you don't have a juicer, you can buy vegetable juices which have been processed at low temperatures from health-food shops.

THE RECIPES

Nut/Seed Mix

Chop equal quantities of three or more kinds of the following nuts and seeds (choose from hazel nuts, almonds, brazil nuts, walnuts, sunflower seeds, pumpkin seeds and sesame seeds) in a coffee grinder, blender or food processor. Keep the mixture in the fridge and use it for muesli or sprinkle it over salads.

Bircher Muesli

2 heaped tablespoons of oat flakes and 1 tablespoon raisins, soaked in ½ cup of water for a couple of hours (best done overnight)
1 tablespoon Nut/Seed Mix
1 apple, grated
2 heaped tablespoons of plain natural yoghurt
squeeze of orange or lemon juice
1–2 teaspoons molasses or honey to sweeten, if desired

Grate the apple and sprinkle with orange or lemon juice to prevent it from oxidizing. Stir in the soaked oat flakes and raisins. Top with yoghurt and sprinkle with the nut/seed mix. Dribble a little honey over the top and serve. You can create wonderful variations on the muesli theme so that it never becomes boring by replacing the apple with other fruit such as pear, banana, pineapple, berries, mango or mixing more than one fruit together. You can even make it with dried fruit which has been soaked overnight in water to plump it up.

Yoghurt Energy Blend

Soak a handful of dried fruit in a bowl with enough water to cover overnight. Select unsulphured sun-dried fruits such as prunes, sultanas, raisins, peaches, pears, apricots and dates. Blend the fruit with a cupful of plain yoghurt and a dash of real vanilla essence in a blender and serve in a tall glass. Or, if you don't have time to soak the dried fruit, blend a banana with the yoghurt instead and add a little honey and a pinch of nutmeg or cinnamon.

Salads

When most people think of salads they groan with boredom at the thought of limp lettuce leaves, cucumber and tomato. What I mean by a salad is nothing less than a symphony of colour and flavour which makes a meal in itself. Add together combinations of vegetables (Chinese leaves, chicory, watercress, white and red cabbage, carrots, radishes, fennel, mushrooms, red and green peppers, Cos lettuce, endive, spring onions, cucumber, celery, Jerusalem artichokes, tomatoes, avocados, kohlrabi etc.) Sprinkle with seeds, nuts, chopped egg or a little grated cheese and toss with a delicious dressing. It can be the beginning of a whole new way of eating. Here are a couple of suggestions to get you started.

Apple Slaw

1 cup white cabbage, finely chopped
1 apple, diced
1 carrot, diced
1–2 sticks celery, diced
a few raisins and a few pecans or walnuts

Combine all the ingredients and dress with an egg mayonnaise to which has been added a teaspoon of wholegrain French mustard and a little water to thin.

Green Drink

Add 1 rounded tablespoon of powdered spirulina and/or
chlorella and/or alfalfa or green barley to a glass of fresh
fruit or vegetable juice and blend well.

Country Salad

1 cup Chinese leaves, shredded
½ red pepper
a little red cabbage, shredded
1 or 2 tomatoes, diced
a few mushrooms, diced
2 spring onions, chopped

Combine the ingredients in a bowl and dress with a
French dressing with plenty of basil and a little garlic.

Special Spinach Salad

A handful of spinach leaves (de-stalked), finely shredded
a few radishes
1 avocado, diced
2 tomatoes, chopped
1 small beetroot, grated (optional)
1 hard-boiled egg, finely chopped

Toss all the ingredients together and dress with a tangy
dressing. Try adding a teaspoon of curry powder to your
ordinary French dressing and blending with a fresh
tomato.

Use the De-stress High-raw regime for three days, then on
Day Six of the *10 Day De-stress Plan* you will be ready to
make the switch to stress-wise eating.

Day Three

Breathe Easy

On Day Three we slip body and breath in gear using a remarkable new kind of yoga – *intrinsic* yoga. According to yogic theory there are three basic sources for the expression of human life: the subconscious or instinctive self, the intellectual or reasoning self, and the *mind* out of which intuition, inspiration and creativity spring. When all three are balanced, stress becomes not a hindrance but a joy, a source of challenge and an invitation to growth.

In most of us they are not balanced. One or another, or even all three are under-developed, over-active or uncontrolled. You have, I am sure, met the kind of person whose intellectual life is particularly vital but whose emotional or instinctual life is undeveloped. Another person may have a capacity for deep feeling but be unable to find expression for it. No matter what the imbalance, it inevitably leads to feelings of frustration and dissatisfaction – two important factors in the development of negative stress. For part of you is either left out of your life or left busy battling against the rest of you instead of being lived. That is where the right kind of yoga can play an important role – intrinsic yoga.

43

Yoga from Within

The meaning of the word yoga is *union* – or, in modern terms, *integration*. Intrinsic yoga is taught by a teacher of unusual gentleness and great skill named Marilyn Mason. It is called intrinsic because it is a kind of yoga that arises from within through the breath rather than being imposed upon your body from outside. For many years I was interested in yoga and yet often bored by yoga classes filled with people standing on their heads and showing how accomplished they are. It always seemed to me that yoga needed to be more internal if it were to help bring about real integration. Yet only when I came upon Marilyn Mason's intrinsic yoga did I begin to experience this. A down-to-earth woman who radiates strength and serenity, her approach is deceptively simple yet suitable for virtually anyone, whether you have been practising yoga for many years or have never done any in your life. She evolved the techniques you will find below out of many influences and experiences, and she is a true master of her craft, yet she insists that her work is forever evolving. She delights in quoting George Bernard Shaw who said: 'I am not a teacher, only a fellow traveller of whom you asked the way – I pointed ahead – ahead of myself as well as you.'

This form of yoga works through the body to restore balance and remove energy blocks and chronic tensions. Intrinsic yoga is not about the *accomplishment* of the exercise or 'asana' you are practising. It is concerned with increasing your *awareness* of the experience in your body and with helping you explore a sense of being at ease. Intrinsic yoga is also about what happens along the way – how you *feel* about an exercise and how *you* experience it. Each exercise is done from *within* with your mind focused upon your breath. Because your body is working in unison with the breath, you begin gradually to experience a new sense of wholeness – the kind of integration of mind, body and breath that lies at the very core of yogic practice. You also gradually develop an inner peace, a feeling of wellbeing and of relaxation that leads to an ability to keep things in perspective, so you can step back and view your life more objectively. Then what once seemed so bad often becomes something you can handle with ease.

Let's Get Started

One of the fundamental aims of yoga is to improve the condition of the spine, which the ancient yogis considered to be our life axis. All the exercises here aim to do this. They begin by centring on the breath. Breath is the key to relaxation. If your breathing is rapid you cannot be relaxed. If your breathing is relaxed you cannot be tense – your heart rate slows (good for high blood pressure), the entire system slows down and you become relaxed in mind and body. At the beginning when Marilyn Mason asks people to concentrate on their breath, many try to change it. She encourages us not to, especially if you suffer from high blood pressure, suggesting instead that we simply be aware of our breathing, aware of the cool air entering the nostrils and the warm air leaving them, or simply that we tune into the rhythm of our breathing without altering it. As you become aware of the breath your out-breath begins to lengthen naturally and makes you feel relaxed. You feel your shoulders becoming a little heavier, and then the rest of your body.

So now let's begin. Never strain in any of the exercises. Always stop if you feel discomfort. If in doubt about anything, seek medical advice before beginning. The movements of intrinsic yoga are designed to follow one another gracefully all the while building on your breath.

45

You will find the practice below is divided into three stages: Stage One begins on Day Three and goes through to Day Five of the *10 Day De-stress Plan.* Stage Two builds upon Stage One by adding new movements. It is to be practised from Day Six through to Day Eight. Finally Stage Three is added on Day Nine, giving you a complete programme for use from then on. The exercises which follow are written so that they can be read out loud by a friend or put on tape if you like until you learn them since it can be difficult to practice and exercise while attempting to read it from a book. They are deceptively simple yet infinitely profound simply because they work so closely with the breath – that great interface between your inner and outer world, each breath gently flowing into the next.

Relaxation Position

Lie on the floor in a relaxation position. It may seem strange to ask you to lie on the floor to relax instead of on a bed but it is only on a firm surface that the body can relax fully. Be aware of the symmetry of your body – visualize an imaginary centre line. Sense that your limbs radiate out from that line as you stretch out your legs and take your arms equally away from the sides of your body –

palms upwards. Having straightened out your legs, you may well be aware of an arching or hollowing under the lower spine. This often happens so bend your knees and rest them together, taking your feet far enough apart so that the knees can stay propped against each other without effort. Now feel your lower back as it gently flattens on the ground. If you still feel tension in the lower back, tilt your pelvis a little, tipping the pubic bone up towards the ceiling, and letting the muscles and the hips relax once more. You should now feel that the lower back is eased as much towards the ground as is comfortable for you. Close your eyes. Relax your jaw, separating your teeth and letting your tongue rest behind the lower teeth.

Now be aware of the back of your neck. It should be long, with your chin drawn gently down towards your chest. This may be a strange feeling in the beginning but it will gradually allow the back of your neck to relax into a beneficial position. Your arms are away from your sides, palms upwards. This lets your shoulders soften. Be aware of the weight of your shoulders as they begin to relax – there is usually a great deal of tension held in the shoulder region. Feel them softening and drifting towards the ground.

As your body begins to let go, stop for a moment to see if there are any other areas of tension. Imagine that you can physically breathe into each of these areas. Then, as you breathe out, visualize the tension evaporating on your out-breath. This is a very useful method of relieving pain or discomfort in any area of your body – even butterflies in the stomach. And, once you get the hang of it, you can create it any time.

Now bring your right hand in to rest over your left collar bone and sense the breath coming in or out gently under your hand. This has the effect of taking the air to the uppermost part of your lungs, where stale pockets of air tend to accumulate through lack of use. Concentrate only on the in-breath for four breaths. Now bring your left hand in to rest over your navel, and be aware of breathing out from beneath that hand. As you breathe out gently draw your tummy muscles inwards and upwards under the rib cage to allow the outward breath to leave the lowest part of your lungs. Try to keep your breathing relaxed, concentrating on the next four out-breaths, and afterwards equally on both in- and out-breaths. As you observe your breathing, you will find that there is a natural pause between the changes of breath. Enjoy that pause and wait until your body is ready to breathe in or out again. Stay centred on your breathing. Although it may be difficult to get the feel of it at first, this kind of centred breathing should be practised as much as possible, for once you begin to experience it you can use it at any time or in any place to relax you. Now return your arms to the floor and you are ready to begin intrinsic yoga.

Stage One

Flamingo

Focusing on your breath, when you next breathe out, draw up your tummy muscles, and slowly ease the right knee towards your chest during the out-breath. As you breathe in, reach up for your knee and hold onto it. On your next out-breath, again pull up your tummy muscles and, without using your hands, ease the knee towards your chest, then use your hands to ease it a little further. Start your in-breath and then soften the grip on that knee, exhale – tummy muscles – moving the knee towards your chest again using your hands. Inhaling, soften the grip, then do one more movement in the same three stages – the breath, move the knee, lastly using your hands. Now, when you are next ready to inhale, release the knee and return your foot to the floor with your knee bent again. Now do the the same on the left side. Exhale, drawing up the tummy muscles, bend your left knee towards your chest, and, inhaling, hold onto the knee. Follow the same procedure, exhaling – in three stages again – no strain, softening the grip, inhaling and so on for three breaths. *Concentrate on the effect of the breath on your movement* rather than achieving it. As you draw your right knee down, you are exerting pressure on the ascending colon, and on the descending colon with the left knee, which acts as a tonic to the digestive system, excellent for a sluggish colon or constipation. Return your foot to the ground on an in-breath.

Now work with both knees in exactly the same way. After drawing up the tummy muscles while exhaling, tip both knees towards the chest, and so on. You will find there is very limited movement of the knees without using your hands. Work with three breaths, and return your feet inhaling. Separate your feet, leaning your knees together,

and check that the lower back is eased down, or again tilt your pelvis as before. Return your arms to the sides of your body, keeping your concentration on your breathing, and checking that the back of your neck is still lengthened.

Rainbow

With palms down, arms at your sides, when you are next ready to breathe, slowly take your arms up towards the ceiling and then start to soften them, bending at the elbows so that they come over to rest on the floor well away from the sides of your head. Check that your elbows and the backs of your wrists actually touch the ground. If not, move your elbows further down towards your feet until they do. When you are ready to exhale, gently straighten the arms in the air once more, and slowly return them to your sides in time with your out-breath. Observe the natural pause between the breaths, keep your chin down, and continue to work for six more breaths. While doing the exercise not

50

only will you be softening your shoulders, you will also be relaxing mentally through the discipline of working your mind, body and breath together in unison.

Shoulder Bridge

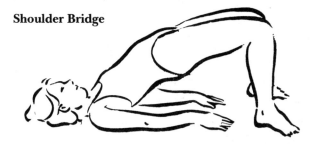

Having finished the Rainbow now take the feet and knees to hip-width to ensure that you don't strain the muscles of the back or abdomen. As you inhale, lift your breastbone and then very gently allow your hips to come off the ground – just a small, gentle lift, not too high. When you are ready to exhale, gently draw up the tummy muscles and slowly lower the middle spine to the ground, and then allow the rest of the spine to ease down, and the back of the neck again to lengthen. Pause there, relax

Dormouse

your chest and, holding onto them, relax into the dormouse position. You might like to rock gently from side to side just to massage your back muscles and coax them to relax. Lower your feet when you are ready, and adopt the relaxation position again.

Crocodile – Variation No.1

Lying on the floor knees bent, bring your feet together, pressing the knees and ankles together. Take your arms away from your sides, palms down. Imagine that you have a coin between your knees and another between your ankles which you need to keep there. When you exhale, draw up your tummy muscles, and very slowly ease your knees out towards the right, both knees absolutely level so that the left foot comes off the floor almost immediately. Be sure to keep your left shoulder down. Inhaling

under your collar bones, slowly return your knees to the centre. Exhale – tummy muscles – lower the knees to the left, right foot coming clear of the ground this time and right shoulder staying down. Don't aim to lower your knees too far. Instead concentrate on the knees staying level and together. Pause for a moment before inhaling again and returning your knees to the centre. Work with two more breaths to each side unless there is any discomfort. If you are not sure if your knees are level, glance down at them to check. Relax with each out-breath, feeling the effect of the exercise on your body – the gentle stretch down the sides of your body, and the rotation in the lower spine. When you finish the movements, ease your knees towards your chest once again, letting the muscles along the spine soften and relax. Release your knees, and separate your feet into the relaxation position again.

Crocodile – Variation No.2

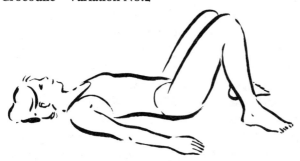

When your muscles have relaxed, separate your knees and your feet to at least hip-width. This time you will be doing a movement similar to the previous one, but aiming to rotate different areas of the spine to ease away tension. We all accumulate tension along the spine, partly through poor posture and partly through sitting in badly designed chairs that exert downward pressure on the spine. That pressure and tension need to be relieved to keep the spine healthy.

First tune into your breath. Your arms should be away from your sides, palms down. Your in-breath is under your collar bones and the out-breath from the abdominal area. As you draw your tummy muscles up, breathe out slowly and ease both knees towards the ground on the right-hand side. Check that your feet are far enough

apart not to inhibit the lowering, or allowing the legs to touch. The left shoulder stays down on the ground. Pause and, when you are ready to inhale slowly, return your knees to the vertical position. Exhale – tummy muscles – lowering both knees towards the left. Feel it working on your outer hip joints and thigh muscles as well as rotating the spine. Inhaling, return your knees again. Work twice more to each side – again only if comfortable – observing the pauses and softening the muscles during the pauses, especially after the exhalation. Experience the movement and its effect as well as the relaxation that follows it. When you finish the exercise, take your knees to your chest yet again, rocking in a circular motion if it feels good, or even in a figure of eight to ensure the massage reaches your sides and the base of your spine.

Unsupported Cobra
Roll over onto your stomach, bringing your arms back to your sides with your palms up and your toes turning inwards, so that your legs roll gently outwards, with your 'comfortable' cheek turned to the floor, i.e. the side you instinctively turn your head to. Be aware of relaxing, of your shoulders softening, and aware of the base of the spine as it relaxes and eases. Aim to take your breath down to the base of your spine, taking energy into that area, and breathing away any tension. The muscles of the lower spine are softening.

The most important point to remember during this

exercise is to keep the back of your neck long and relaxed. One of our greatest mistakes in modern life is to shorten the back of the neck. When we are driving cars we all tend to lift our chins – particularly women who often have difficulty seeing over the bonnet otherwise. The design of much modern furniture also makes us shorten the back of the neck which can cause headaches, migraines and stress that spreads into the shoulders and eventually transmits to the spine. You can often improve these problems (even what appears to be a totally separate back problem) by simply lengthening the back of your neck, and taking that awareness into everyday life, not just when you are practising yoga.

Now bring your forehead to the floor, with your palms down at your sides. Your feet need to be hip-width apart. You will be extending the crown of your head forward as you inhale so that the back of your neck stays long as you lift. When you are ready to inhale, extend the crown forward and then upwards a little as you lift your head and shoulders only as much as you are comfortable with, keeping your arms passive at your sides. When you are ready to exhale, slowly lower and relax, turning your less

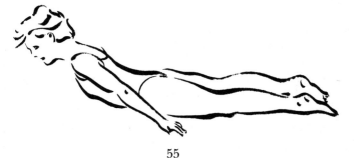

comfortable cheek to the floor. Allow the muscles to relax at the back of your neck, your shoulders and your spine. Observe your breath. If the movement is a strain rest, otherwise when you are ready, once more return your forehead to the floor. Extend the crown as you inhale, and begin to lift your head and the shoulders – chin down. Ease down exhaling, and once more turn your comfortable cheek to the floor, palms upwards, toes inwards and heels falling outwards. Allow all the muscles you have been using to relax, and feel your breathing returning to normal.

Very gently roll over onto your back again. To compensate for the cobra movement bring your knees to your chest in the dormouse position and either rest with your knees above your chest or rock gently – feeling the spine 'alive', warm and relaxed. The cobra is also a tonic for the respiratory system and good for asthma sufferers – as indeed is all the breath awareness of intrinsic yoga.

When you feel the muscles have softened, keep your knees above your chest with your arms gently around them, and exhaling – tummy muscles – draw both knees closer to your chest as you did in the Flamingo. Then, keeping your knees drawn towards your chest after exhaling, inhale, being aware of the abdominal massage. Exhaling, relax the muscles but do not soften the grip, and take one more inhalation, relax again exhaling, and release your knees inhaling. Separate your feet into the Relaxation Position, chin drawn downwards, and focusing on your breath while it slows down.

Rainbow/Shoulder Bridge

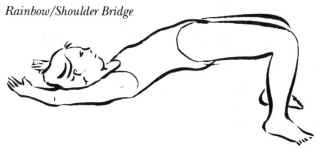

This is the end of Stage One for Days Three and Four of the *10 Day De-stress Plan*. During the second stage, which begins on Day Five, the Rainbow and Shoulder Bridge may be joined into one flowing movement if desired, and the variations of the Crocodile can also be modified as follows:

Stage Two

Crocodile – Variation No.1 *(Extended Version)*

Tune into your breathing again, centring yourself, your in-breath under the collar bones, out-breath drawing the tummy muscles upwards. The pauses become evident, and also the feeling of great peace, of being in the

momentary stillness before the breath changes. The feet and knees are pressed together as before. Exhale – tummy muscles – slowly lowering both knees towards the right,

keeping the left shoulder down, but the left foot leaves the ground. Return, inhaling, and repeat to the left in the same way. After returning to the centre on an in-breath, work again to the right but, if you are comfortable, stay in position for up to three breaths initially, being aware of your breathing. Feel your spine gently lengthen, as you inhale under the collar bones, and the muscles soften as you exhale – even in this twisted position. Make sure the knees stay level and together. Return when you are ready, inhaling and, if you are happy, work to the left again in the same way. Experience the movement and the breath. When you return to the centre, take your knees to your chest again and listen to your body as to whether you should rock gently or not. Return to the Relaxation Position in your own time, and feel the warmth in the muscles you have been working. Let that warmth soften the muscles still more. Observe your breath slowing down and relax.

Crocodile – Variation No.2 *(Extended Version)*

In the next crocodile movement your knees and your feet must be well apart. The same extension applies as for the previous version, i.e. holding the position for a maximum of three breaths initially, using the breath to relax into the exercise, and becoming conscious of where you feel the breathing in your body. As with the previous

extension, only stay in position if you are comfortable and return to centre on an in-breath. After the exercise, yet again, take your knees to your chest, and relax, perhaps rocking in a circular motion or a figure of eight to massage the muscles. Explore the feeling in the muscles along your spine, and out towards your sides as you rock. Return to the Relaxation Position in your own time and check that the lower spine is eased down. If not, tip the pelvis as before. Relax.

Half-Scissor

At this stage we are going to add in one more exercise which will work towards the very base of the spine. It is particularly beneficial for sufferers of sciatica, as it helps to relieve tension in this area, but it must be used very gently and only gradually built up if you feel it is helpful for you.

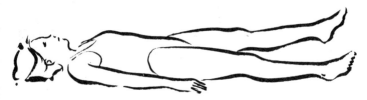

Tune into your breath and straighten out your legs. Arms away from your sides, palms down. When you are ready to breathe in gently lift the left leg no more than a foot off the ground. As you exhale, cross the left leg over your

right leg towards the floor on your right, keeping your left leg low and both legs straight. When you are ready to inhale, take the leg back to its starting position, keeping it low to the ground and straight. Exhaling, lower it to the ground. When you are doing this exercise you need to roll the hip of the leg you are working up off the ground as much as you can, but always keep both shoulders on the ground. Work with the right leg when you are ready – in four stages. Inhale, lifting the leg a few inches, exhale crossing it over (letting the right hip roll to follow it), right shoulder down. Inhale bringing the leg back, and exhale lowering it to the ground again. Only if it is comfortable repeat the exercise, taking care not to strain, but working in the four stages for each movement. When you are ready, take your knees back to your chest and relax in the dormouse position as before, following your instincts about rocking to ensure the very base of your spine softens – feel the warmth in the muscles.

Stage Three

Stage Three begins on Day Eight of the *10 Day De-stress Plan* and encompasses all of the above but in addition adds the sequence of the Cat movements.

The Cat

This exercise is effective in alleviating backache and stiffness, and digestive discomfort.

Come to a kneeling position (if you have knee problems you can put a folded blanket under your knees or, indeed, practise the same kind of movements while sitting on a chair). You need to have your hands directly under your shoulders, and your knees under your hips. Knees and hands should be shoulder-width apart. Your elbows must be slightly bent throughout the exercise, because to straighten them would create tension in the back of the neck, and to bend them any more would mean they would take too much weight. If the hands become uncomfortable, make fists and turn the knuckles towards the floor. Tune into your breathing pattern and let your spine relax, as well as your neck and shoulders.

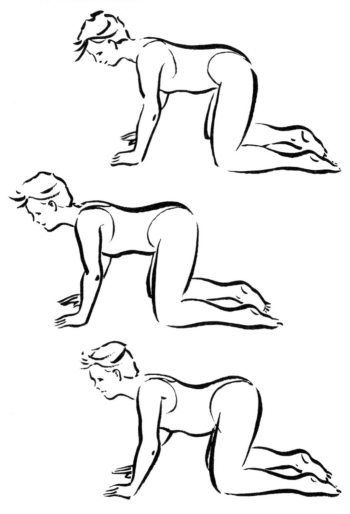

When you are ready to inhale, begin by extending your crown first forward and then upwards just a little, then move your chest down and lastly lift your hips.

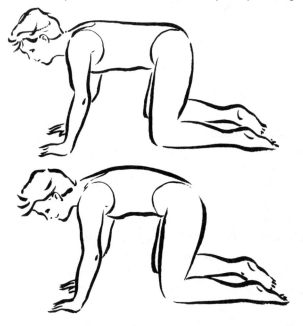

Exhale, drawing up your stomach muscles and tuck your tail under, round the lower back, middle back, then drop your head a little.

Inhale, extending the crown again while the rest of the spine stays still; then your head raises gently, your chest moves down, and your hips lift. Exhale – tummy muscles – tail under, rounding the lower spine, middle then upper spine and lowering your head. Elbows still slightly bent. On the next inhalation extend the crown, allowing the movement to travel down the length of your spine as before until the hips lift. Exhaling, the movement moves up the length of your spine until your head lowers. Lean your hips back towards your heels just until the stretch reaches your upper back – elbows still bent.

Inhale, extend the crown and again feel the movement travel down your spine, and exhale once more as the movement travels up your spine and lean your hips back

64

again. If you are comfortable move to one more breath, feeling every inch of your spine moving with every breath. When you finish, lie back down and for the last time take your knees to your chest and feel the muscles softening along the length of your spine. When they have relaxed, once more adopt the Relaxation Position and rest for a minute or two, feeling all tension slip away from your body. It is a good idea to practice the Cat in front of a mirror, as often we are not aware that an area of the spine is not moving as it should until it can be seen working.

When you feel ready to come up to a standing position, do so very slowly and then take a few deep breaths. Always stretch gently – particularly if you are going to drive soon after your practice – just to make sure you are not too relaxed to concentrate!

After your *10 Day De-stress Plan* has finished, try to lay aside a special time for yoga. I like to do my yoga in the evening as it is so relaxing. Other people prefer first thing in the morning. Try to practice a little every day, even if it is only for five minutes. You can begin to feel more peaceful and centred very quickly. It has been said that the rise of yoga in the West is directly attributable to the instant benefit felt from very little practice. Marilyn Mason encourages people to dedicate a regular time of day to their practice, and to announce to the family or whoever is around them that this is *their* time. Take the phone off the hook. Forget to answer the door. Then people will learn to respect this time. At first they may think you are a bit strange to want to isolate yourself in this way, but when they begin to notice a greater peace emanating from you (which has spin-off effects on those around you), they become happy to give you that space – and to reap its benefits.

Chill Out

Day Four of the *10 Day De-stress Plan* is full of magic – the magic that begins to transform fear into challenge and powerlessness into freedom. And the amazing thing about it all is that the place in which this metamorphosis takes place lies deep within.

We live in a world of constant activity. It is a world of striving and goals, of planning and remembering – a world of never-ending sensory stimulation, ideas and discoveries. Yet amidst all this activity somewhere inside you is a centre of stillness – a wordless, formless space – the home of your self or your soul. There seeds of creativity are sown which later become your ideas and your accomplishments. There in the silence and the darkness you can begin to listen to your own 'inner voice'. You can come to know the difference between what you really want, feel and think, and what has been programmed into you by habits, false notions and other people's values. This space – your centre – is also a place of safety and security. You can move out of it, as you choose, to meet the outside world, form friendships, love and learn. Yet it is a permanent sanctuary to which you can always return when you feel overburdened, tired, confused or in need of new vitality and direction. Locating this centre within yourself, recognizing its value, and living your life more and more from it makes you a stress-hardy person. It is also an essential part of staying well. The key that opens this particular door for most of us is *relaxation*.

Passive Awareness

By relaxation, I don't mean sleeping, or flopping down on a bed when you feel you can't go on, or losing yourself in a mindless state in front of the television – although sleep is certainly essential and the other two states have things to recommend them too. I mean something far more: learning to move *at will* into a state of deep stillness in which your usual concerns, your habitual thoughts, and the never-ending activity of your daily life are replaced by alert – yet totally *passive* – awareness. Dipping into such a state even for a few minutes allows many of the physiological changes normally experienced during sleep to take place while your body and mind are revitalized. But it is different from sleep. For while your body is passive, your mind is highly alert.

For some people this state occurs spontaneously – often between sleep and wakefulness. It is during this time that their best ideas come and that they experience a sense of harmony both within themselves and in relation to the rest of the world. Scientists studying a state of psychophysical relaxation find that the brain-wave patterns in it are very different from those of the normally awake state. After tens of thousands of hours of observation of the changes in brain-wave patterns in subjects hooked up to EEG equipment, researchers have been able to analyse and describe a number of interesting altered states of consciousness that occur during conscious relaxation, each with its own brain-wave patterns, objective physical manifestations and subjective feelings. They have discovered that there is an increase in overall awareness and creativity as a person moves from one level of relaxation into the next deeper one.

Most of us have a fear of letting go, thinking that if we give up control of things we won't be able to think clearly and independently or work well, or that someone is likely to put something over on us. In fact, just the opposite is true. When you are able to enter a state of deep relaxation at will, this *frees* you from patterns of living and thinking to which you tend to be a slave – although usually an unconscious one. It enables you to think more clearly and simply and to act more directly when action is called for. The freedom that comes with this holds within it the magic for transforming negative stressors into exhilarating challenges.

Relief from Stress

Relaxation is also the most important key to mitigating the damaging effects of long-term stress. This is something which by now has been well established scientifically. Many studies have been made of people taught a relaxation technique and then monitored as to the psychological and physiological changes that take place after fifteen or twenty minutes of practising it. These studies show that relaxation techniques bring the parasympathetic branch of the autonomic nervous system into play, calming you, reducing oxygen consumption, lowering blood lactates (high lactate levels are associated with anxiety, arousal and hypertension), slowing your heartbeat significantly and changing brain-wave patterns. They have also shown that repeated practice can lead to improved memory, increased perceptual ability, and a subjective feeling in participants that their work and their lives are more creative and more rewarding than they were before.

Another interesting benefit from the daily practice of deep relaxation is a reduction of negative habits such as drug taking – of both prescription and mind-altering drugs – alcohol consumption and cigarette smoking. Research carried out in the United States involving 2,000 students between the ages of nineteen and twenty-three who had practised a form of meditation for periods of between a few months to a couple of years, showed that their dependence on alcohol, drugs and cigarettes dropped sharply. The number of smokers was reduced by half in the first six months of doing the practice. By twenty-one months it was down to one-third. And these changes were entirely *spontaneous* – at no time was any suggestion made that relaxation or meditation would change any of these habits.

Harvard professor and expert in behavioural medicine, Herbert Benson MD, did the first studies into the effects of Transcendental Meditation many years ago. He has since continued to investigate this state of psychophysical relaxation and has shown that each of us has what he calls the 'relaxation response' – a natural ability to experience the relaxed state with all its benefits. All we need to tap into it is a method to turn it on. The possibilities are many. They range from meditation, yoga, breathing exercises, zazen, silent repetition of a word and autogenic training to steady aerobic exercise and biofeedback. Each can be useful as a tool for silencing everyday thoughts and for temporarily shutting off habitual ways of seeing the world and doing things. Practise one regularly and you build a powerful and useful bridge between your inner and outer world. All of them are different. Some will work better for you or be more enjoyable than others. That is why it is worthwhile to try a few different techniques until you discover which ones you prefer.

Practising one or two techniques every day will make

you aware of the enormous power your own mind has – the power to alleviate suffering and bring a sense of well-being, the power to change those things you want to change but which seemed impossible to change before, the power to expand your whole awareness of your world of work, pleasure and relationships. Meanwhile, almost automatically, you reap the well-documented physical and psychological benefits of stilling your mind. But regular practice is important.

Discipline for Freedom

We live in an age where discipline is often looked down upon as something which interferes with spontaneity and freedom – something old fashioned and stifling to life. We tend to rebel against it. But it has been my experience, as well as the experience of a great many professionals working in the field of humanistic and depth psychology, that the kind of discipline needed for daily practice of meditation or deep relaxation tends – far from stifling one's ability to be involved in the spontaneous business of life – actually to free it. This is something you will have to find out for yourself. At first it may take a little effort to get up fifteen or twenty minutes earlier each morning to practise a technique and to take fifteen minutes out of your busy afternoon or early evening to practise again, but you will find it is well worth it. The most common excuse is that you don't have time. The reality of the situation is that practising twice a day for fifteen to twenty minutes will *give* you time, not take it from you, for you will find that you do everything with greater efficiency and enjoyment, and that far less of your energy is wasted on fruitless activity. Studies show that every minute you spend in a deeply relaxed state yields a fourfold return in the energy you have in your outer life.

Here are a few useful techniques for you to try. Some are orientated more towards the body, others focus more on the mental processes. But it is important to remember that there is no real separation between the two. Mind and body are not different entities, they are merely different ends of the same continuum. Each of these techniques will affect both. It could not be otherwise.

Zazen

One of the simplest ways of meditating, this technique involves nothing more than just being aware of your breathing. But don't be deceived by its simplicity. It is a potent tool for stilling the mind and regenerating the body. And concentrating your awareness on the breath is not as easy as it sounds.

● Find yourself a quiet place where you will not be disturbed. You can sit cross-legged on the floor with a small cushion underneath you or you can sit in a chair if you prefer, but your back should be straight. (This straight-back position is a requirement for many meditation techniques since it creates a physical equilibrium which makes calm mental focus possible.) Let your hands rest quietly in your lap.

● Close your eyes. Take several long, slow breaths, breathing from your abdomen so it swells out with each in-breath and sinks in again when you breathe out.

● Now rock your body from side to side and then around in large, gentle circles from your hips to the top of your head. Rock in increasingly smaller circles until you gradually come to rest in the centre.

71

● Now breathe in and out through your nose quietly without *doing* anything to your breathing – that is, don't try to breathe deeper or slower or faster, just breathe normally. With each out-breath count silently to yourself. So it goes: in-breath, out-breath 'one... in-breath, out-breath 'two... and so on up to ten, counting only on the out-breath. When you get to ten go back and begin again at one. If you lose count halfway, it doesn't matter. Go back and start the count at one again. Counting isn't the point. It is a way of focusing your mind on your breath.

If you are like most people, the first few times you do the exercise you will find you lose count often and you are frequently distracted by thoughts or noises. It makes no difference. It works just as well anyway. Each time some random thought distracts you, simply turn your mind gently back again to counting the breaths. Distractions don't change the effectiveness of the meditation.

● After fifteen minutes – sneak a look at your wrist-watch if you must – stop. Sit still for a moment, then open your eyes and slowly begin to go about your every-day activities again.

The exercise, like most techniques, is best done twice a day, morning and evening. A beginner will usually notice positive results by the end of a week but they become increasingly apparent the longer you go on doing it. Some Buddhist monks do this exercise for two or three years before beginning any other form of meditation.

Benson's Relaxation Response Technique

Herbert Benson, who wrote *The Relaxation Response* and

Maximum Mind, discovered that the same measurable physical benefits accrued from practising any form of meditation which depends on the silent repetition of a mantra – a word-sound. This can be done by repeating *any* word over and over while the eyes are closed and the body is in a quiet state.

Meditation using a mantra has a long tradition. Some mantras are said to be sacred words that have particular sound vibrations which transmit particular powers. Each tradition has its own mantras such as *Guru Om, Om mani padme hum, La ilaha illa 'lla* or, in the Catholic religion, *Hail Mary, full of grace, the Lord is with thee.* Whether their magic aspects are true or not, the technique works beautifully to replace the habitual chatter that runs through one's mind, worries about things past and things yet to come.

Benson suggests you find a word that is pleasing to you. It could be anything, say, 'flower', 'peace', or 'love'. He likes the word 'one' as it is simple and has the connotation of unity about it. The teacher Krishnamurti once remarked that any word would be better than the fruitless and often destructive thoughts that normally run through our minds; then he wryly suggested 'Coca-Cola'. Here's how.

● Find a quiet place where you won't be disturbed for fifteen to twenty minutes and a comfortable chair that supports your back.

● Sit down and close your eyes. Give yourself a moment to settle in and you are ready to begin.

● Simply sit there, feet on the floor and eyes closed, quietly repeating your word over and over to yourself: 'one... one... one...'

● Whenever your mind wanders or you are disturbed by

a sound or thought, simply turn your mind gently back to repeating the word again.

● That is all there is to it. After fifteen to twenty minutes, stop repeating the mantra and get ready to open your eyes.

● Open your eyes, stretch, and go about your everyday activities. This is a particularly useful technique once you have practised it a few times because you can do it in so many different places, such as in a waiting room or on a commuter train or bus. I know a lot of men and women who have made it a part of their daily trek to and from work, with tremendous benefits.

Beyond Relaxation

Once you are familiar with the practice of deep relaxation or meditation and with all the benefits it can bring you, you might be interested to go on to investigate how it can be used to expand the powers of your mind and heighten your creativity and joy. We will look at both on Day Seven. In the meantime begin practising the Chill Out for fifteen to twenty minutes twice a day. In six weeks you will feel like a new person.

Day Five

Move Light

Now it is time to add exercise to the *10 Day De-stress Plan.* But the idea that you should exercise because it enhances your ability to deal with stress is all wrong. Not that exercise will not do this; it certainly will. It is probably the single most important thing you can take up to make you resistant to stress damage. Regular exercise can help you live longer, have more energy, look younger and stay healthier. But anyone who faces a thirty-minute walk, run, swim or cycle as a chore hasn't yet discovered what exercise is all about. Movement, whether it be in the form of running, walking, swimming, yoga, bicycling or other sports, taken regularly over weeks and months, expands your whole world and helps you discover one important truth: that just about anything is possible. If this sounds exaggerated or if this is not what some complex and tedious exercise programme has brought you in the past, then you have a whole new world of enjoyment and experience just waiting to be discovered.

Your Body Thrives on Motion

The human body, which we often treat like a machine, is

in reality nothing of the sort. Unlike a machine, which wears out with use, the more your body is used, the stronger, more resistant to stress and more expressive it becomes. Most people tend to ignore their body and its needs. Or they treat it in a narcissistic way – more like an object to be pushed and pummelled and pampered than a living thing. Many of the exercise programmes you find in books and magazines have been geared to this attitude – callisthenics designed for the self-obsessed who spend hours doing some boring movement in the hope that it will whittle away another inch from their right thigh, something which seems of prime importance although probably nobody else will notice. This attitude really misses the point.

In part it comes about as a result of our culture. Seldom is the body recognized as the simple physical expression of the person – an inseparable part of him or her and, as such, a vehicle by which to communicate and respond to life, to experience pleasure and pain, and a means of relating intimately with our environment. If your feelings about your body and your relationship with it are not as intimate and as at ease as this it probably means you are not experiencing life fully. It is also quite likely that you are not using your mental and creative abilities as successfully as you could. Regular exercise brings a feeling of being intensely alive, along with greater self-confidence and a lively sense of play that comes from knowing you are able to meet each new challenge in your life spontaneously with openness and enthusiasm. This knowledge is fundamental to making a positive experience of stress. Once you discover this for yourself, then far from being something you do quickly to get it over with – a chore you virtuously suffer because you know it is doing you good – any exercise you do will become one of the most enjoyable parts of your life. American cardiologist Dr George

Sheehan has done much to make people aware of the essential nature of exercise. Sheehan says: 'Exercise that is not play accentuates rather than closes the split between body and spirit. Exercise that is drudgery, labour, something done only for the final result is a waste of time.' Moving freely down a country road at dawn, gliding through water, speeding down mountains covered with fine snow are things that you will do for their own sake, for the pleasure of it. The fact that these activities are good for you in time becomes incidental to the lovely unexpected pleasure. When this happens then you will have discovered for yourself what exercise is really all about.

Movement Gives You Energy

Many of us don't function at anywhere near peak. We tire easily. We feel under strain and look for any escape from fatigue. When the body is under stress it produces large quantities or adrenalin – the powerful hormone that is a chemical product of the sympathetic nervous system. Adrenalin is an emergency hormone which mobilizes the body for fight or flight, giving extra power when it is needed most. It increases your heartbeat, calls forth sugar reserves and causes your muscles to contract. In modern life the adrenalin produced through emotional and physical stress is not all used up as often as it should be in physical movement. Instead, it is stored in your heart and brain, a phenomenon known as the adrenalin build-up. When this build-up is great, as it often is in city dwellers, the efficiency of your heart decreases while excess adrenalin in your brain adversely affects your moods and emotions, making you feel tired, irritable and at the end of your tether.

Exercise calls forth any stores of adrenalin, dispersing them into the system, burns the adrenalin up and so clears away the build-up, resulting in a renewed feeling of vigour and freshness. This is why after a hard day when you feel completely exhausted or very irritable, if you can resist the temptation to collapse on the sofa and instead take exercise, you will be amazed to find that in about thirty minutes your energy returns.

But there are other reasons for the increase in energy that sedentary people experience when they take up regular exercise. When you exercise regularly, changes occur in the cells of your body. There is an increase in the number of mitochondria, the microscopic factories in each cell where energy is produced. This creates more sites for the production of an energy-rich compound called adenosine triphosphate (ATP), so the quantities of this mitochondrial enzyme increase and it is produced more rapidly than before.

Exercise Improves Your Mood

The stress-protective effect that exercise has on your mental and emotional state is well known. Ask anyone who in the past couple of years has taken up running or another vigorous activity and he will tell you that it has brought him enhanced mental energy and concentration plus a feeling of heightened mental activity. Some claim too that, as a result of beginning to work out, they discover a sense of willpower they didn't know they had. It seems to pervade your whole life, making it possible for you to carry through arduous tasks or bear with difficult situations without becoming discouraged even when you are fatigued. Taking a long walk or going for a swim or cycle or run helps clear away anxiety and mental confusion as you give over to the rhythm of movement, particularly if you can exercise in the open air, in a park or other pleasant surroundings.

A number of studies have also shown that vigorous exercise taken regularly alters one's mood for the better and is capable of bringing about a long-term sense of wellbeing. Professor Tom Curetin at the University of Illinois studied 2,500 sedentary people who took up exercise. He discovered that they quickly developed significantly greater energy and less tension than they had when the study began. Herbert de Vries at the University of Southern California looked at stress levels and muscle tension in subjects who had either been given tranquillizers or who engaged in physical exercise every day. He found that as little activity as even a fifteen-minute walk is more relaxing and efficient in dealing with stress than a course of tranquillizers. At the University of Arizona Medical School, psychologist William P. Morgan discovered that exercise significantly lowers anxiety levels. In another interesting study, psychiatrist John Greist experimented with depressed university students, treating some with conventional psychotherapy and asking others to run for a few minutes each day. After ten weeks he found that the runners felt significantly better, studied better and did better in their exams than the conventionally treated group. Many forward-thinking psychologists now successfully treat a variety of emotional disorders by getting their patients to run or take long walks. They also find exercise useful in helping drug addicts and alcoholics to kick the habit.

Science is not yet able to explain fully why these positive mental effects come about from simply exercising regularly but many believe that they are at least in part related to increased levels of a hormone called noradrenaline or norepinephrine in the brain. This is a hormone essential for your brain's messages to be transmitted along certain nerves in the body. People with high blood levels of noradrenaline tend to be cheerful

79

and happy, while those who suffer from moodiness and depression show low levels. Taking up regular exercise can help turn moodies into true cools. Another possible contributor may be its ability to increase the blood supply to the brain so that brain and nerve tissue receive more oxygen, enabling all the cells to function better. Exercise also improves your ability to sleep deeply. Studies show that people who are relatively free of emotional conflicts and depression sleep deeply, while at least 85 per cent of those with psychological disturbances have long-term insomnia in one form or another.

Positive Addiction

Many researchers into sports have commented on the ability regular strenuous exercise has to develop qualities of courage and character as well as greater physical stamina – both important factors in being able to handle stress well. Some believe that this is because regular strenuous movement is a natural *need* of human beings, one for which we have been genetically programmed and one which, if denied over a period of time, leads to feelings of timidity, negativity, lack of creativity and chronic fatigue as well as physical illness. Psychiatrist William Glasser, author of *Positive Addiction*, and others have noticed that once people become regularly involved in an exercise programme for several weeks and months, they develop a kind of addiction to it that replaces many of the negative habits they had before they started, whether it be the excessive use of alcohol, smoking or self-deprecating thoughts and unproductive behaviour in relationships.

It is certainly true that once you discover the joy of exercise, and the feelings of wellbeing and mental and physical freedom that come with it and carry over into the rest of your life, you don't want to give it up. Meanwhile the negative addictions tend gradually to disappear, almost automatically. You almost never meet a swimmer or runner who smokes, although many did before they took up the sport. The whole process of eliminating negative addictions appears to be quite simple and to require no great effort of will. It is just that the pleasurable feedback you get from the habit of over-eating or smoking in no way approaches the sense of exuberance and satisfaction that exercise brings. And since cigarettes interfere with running by making it harder for you to breathe, and over-eating interferes by making you feel sluggish and creating more weight to carry about, you find – even unconsciously – that you no longer want to sustain your negative habits. They are just not as satisfying as the positive ones. This is something that large numbers of people have experienced, and something that I know firsthand because it happened to me.

Key to Personal Growth

We live in a culture that puts increasing emphasis on the use of human potential and individual growth. Regular exercise can contribute to both in no small measure thanks to its ability to enhance self-esteem. This, by the way, has nothing to do with self-centredness or selfishness. A high degree of self-esteem forms the foundation of security that enables you to form a positive relationship with stressors in your life. Self-esteem also protects you from stress damage and helps prevent the development of long-term serious illness. For many years research showed that the ambitious, so-called type A personalities – especially those who tend to be hostile and suspicious – are in much greater danger of heart-attacks than their more complacent, so-called type B neighbours. The latest investigations into personality characteristics and their effect on stress and health has taken a fascinating new twist. Studies by researchers recently reported in *Behavioural Medicine* show that the greatest personality 'protector' against the ravages of heart disease may not be an ability to relax and stay cool, as was once believed, but rather a high degree of self-esteem. The new research shows that while driven ambitious type A people with low self-esteem are highly at risk from stress damage, those type A personalities with a high sense of self-worth are greatly protected by the ability they have to focus all of their creative dynamic energies on whatever they are doing at any particular time.

Regular exercise can be a major factor in enhancing self-esteem and it has a very special way of doing it too. For all of the changes in you which happen when you exercise regularly come from *within* and are tightly integrated with your total personality. They are not just some kind of 'positive' thinking imposed upon you from the outside. These findings about self-esteem came at a time when an official government committee investigating the importance of self-esteem in California had just released a report on the subject. Their definition of self-esteem was, 'Appreciating my own worth and importance and having the character to be accountable to myself and to act responsibly to others.' The committee reported that self-esteem and personal responsibility are key issues in the re-creation of a healthy society out of one which has been warped and unsupported by criminal justice, educational and social systems, all of which, by their very nature, undermine personal power.

My own experience and that of other physically active people is that there is nothing that brings quite such a sense of confidence as getting into a regular routine of exercise, even if this means nothing more than parking your car half a mile or a mile from where you work and walking the rest of the way, or climbing six or eight flights of steps instead of taking a lift, or going to a gym three or four times a week to work out with weights for three-quarters of an hour. The thing that matters about experiencing the uplifting benefits of exercise is that you keep doing it regularly. Your body is a very dense medium yet it has a remarkable ability to transform itself. Such transformation takes time. It is the repetition of movement, whether it be walking, running, swimming, weight training, tennis or whatever other activity you choose, that re-aligns the body, re-balances the biochemistry, creates a sense of heightened self-esteem and brings a feeling that you are in control of your own life – able to make conscious choices to do whatever you want to do. You can't get better protection from stress-caused damage than that.

Transcendental Movement

In many ways the most interesting result of exercise in relation to becoming stress-wise lies in its ability to create a stillness of mind and inner peace that is usually only associated with meditation and which was, until recently at least, considered the exclusive province of religion. In *The Psychic Side of Sports* Michael Murphy and Rhea A. White draw strong parallels between the experiences of mystics and the descriptions athletes have given of altered states of consciousness that happened on the road or playing field. Commenting on the fact that until now we have been scarcely aware of the parallels because athletes tend not to talk about this kind of experience, they say:

> There are probably several good reasons for this, among them a wisdom about talking the spiritual side of athletics to death and a refusal

to build up false expectations about it. The athletes' silence about these matters is not unlike the old Zen Buddhist attitude: if you experience illumination while chopping wood, keep chopping wood. If there is something in the act that invited ecstasy, it doesn't need an extra hype or some benediction. And there is a wisdom in letting people discover these experiences in their own way, for too many expectations can dampen the spontaneity and sense of release that are part of sport's glory. They can take the fun out of sports in the name of religion.

This sums up well my own feeling about exercise. It really is something you need to find out about for yourself by doing it, for in the last analysis words are dead – only symbols used to describe an experience which can never be conveyed by description.

Getting Started

Before beginning any exercise programme it is best to check up on how fit you are *now*. If you are over thirty-five or suffer from high blood pressure, have a family history of heart disease or are recovering from an illness, you should have a check-up with your doctor to be sure that what you are planning to do is safe for you.

In the past few years a number of complicated tests for cardiac and pulmonary strength have been devised by our ever more high-technology medicine. Most of them are expensive and unnecessary – that is unless you happen to be recovering from a heart attack. Do you need a ECG stress test first? Probably not. They are not only over-practised and over-priced, they are also by no means the perfect indicator of heart trouble that we have been led to believe. In one study of people with heart disease who were given an electrocardiographic stress test, as many as 62 per cent of them showed up normal, while in another study 47 per cent of those who showed up abnormal in the testing did *not* have heart disease. Although the ECG is far from foolproof it is certainly useful in determining a person's state of health. If you have any of these warning signs, it is a good idea to see your doctor and get his approval for any exercise programme you are planning.

- Are you short of breath at even the mildest exertion?
- Do you ever have pain in your legs when you walk which goes away when you rest?
- Do you often have swelling in the ankles?
- Have you ever been told that you have heart disease?
- Do you get chest pain when you perform any strenuous activity?

If you have none of these warning signs, there is a simple way to check yourself out for fitness.

Take a Walk

Walk a brisk two miles in thirty minutes. How do you feel afterwards? Do you have any nausea or dizziness? No? Then so long as you have no medical condition that indicates caution, you are probably fit enough to start at the bottom of a slow, graded exercise programme. If, however, you have any difficulties on the walk, then keep up this two-mile walk until such time as you can do it easily in half an hour before you start doing anything more strenuous – you will be surprised at how rapidly your condition improves even from daily walking. Don't get discouraged, just keep things up and you will soon be running.

Brisk daily walks can not only be a lot of fun, they can be a major factor in disease prevention as they help keep your body clean from the inside out while increasing your vitality and improving your mental state. How far? How fast? That depends on how fit you are already. Start slowly if you are not used to exercise, and then gradually – over several weeks if necessary – work up your pace to 4 m.p.h. That means you will be walking a mile in about 15 minutes. Once you can do that easily you will be able to walk, say, three miles a day in 45 minutes and you'll be getting a very pleasant but effective aerobic workout which will bring you lots of energy and have you feeling great.

Of course, there are other options – you could swim or jog or skip or rebound on one of the mini-trampolines which are particularly good for stimulating internal spring-cleaning. But each of these things requires special equipment and special places or times to do, whereas walking can be done almost anywhere by anyone without any special training and without spending extra money.

Make a pact with yourself to walk for 45 minutes a day – rain or shine – for the next five days of *10 Day De-stress Plan*. If you have young children, take them with you in the pram or pushchair. Older children can benefit as much from exercise as you do. If the weather is bad then just make sure you are all equipped with waterproofs or warm clothing. Or you can get up early before anyone else is awake and go out by yourself (this is my favourite time for exercising). If you go out to work, carry your work shoes with you and wear a comfortable pair of trainers: take the bus or the tube to within a couple of miles of your workplace and walk from there. You can change back into the dress shoes once you are at work. How old you are, how overweight you are, how out of condition you may be now matters little so long as you follow the step-by-step approach and have your doctor's approval.

86

Where you are *now* and where you will be *then* – in three, six or twelve months' time – are completely different.

Creating Energy

The experience of gaining energy from walking or any other aerobic activity is a common one. You will have it too. And there are things you can do to enhance it. For instance, each day before you begin your activity, be aware of your body as an energy factory by focusing your attention at a point a couple of inches below your navel. This is known as the 'hara' centre. If you are able to think of your *self* as emanating from it – not just when you are exercising but whenever you need energy – you will find this releases a great deal of vitality. This technique is traditionally used for creating powerful yet controlled movements for the Oriental disciplines such as aikido, tai chi, and even Japanese and Chinese calligraphy. The hara, located in the abdomen, has always been considered a centre of power – like a smouldering furnace in which the fire is forever waiting to burst into flame. As you begin your movements, keep focusing on this area and make every movement as though it comes from here.

When you are walking, running or swimming, bicycling or rowing, focus on the hara centre, gradually increasing the speed and force of your movements until your find your own pace. It should be one that makes enough physical demand on you – you can check that by your pulse – but not so much that you are left gasping for breath. Then you are ready to get into the second energy game which is great for stress-wisdom, that of being *here* and *now*.

87

Here and Now

Almost everyone has experienced the ability to summon up energy to cope with particularly demanding situations – getting a second wind when you have been up all night nursing a sick child and thought you couldn't possibly drag even one more ounce of strength from yourself... having an all-encompassing fatigue somehow disappear into thin air with the unexpected arrival of a much-loved friend you haven't seen for years... discovering the extra strength that an athlete gets at the end of a long race when he feels he has already given all he has. What, more than anything else, determines how much energy you have in any of these situations is not your physical strength, not what you ate for lunch, nor even how much sleep you had the night before. It is simply whether or not you are *totally involved* in what you are doing – physically, mentally and emotionally. This is the theory of biologists, sports experts and psychologists who have looked seriously at the phenomenon of energy or vitality and tried to distinguish between the traits of those people with high energy levels and the rest of us. They find that all high-energy people, whether they are athletes, executives, artists or whoever, have one thing in common: *total involvement.* Learning this kind of focus or total involvement is an excellent way of turning what could be a stressful experience into a creative one.

For most of us this kind of complete involvement – although it is fundamental to making a creative experience of the way you handle stress – doesn't come naturally. It probably did when we were children, but it is an ability we have since lost. While you are exercising is an excellent time to re-learn it. While you are moving, pay attention to your surroundings – the sights, the smells, the feel of the air – and to your own inner sensations.

88

Visualize something in graceful motion such as a horse or antelope, a dolphin or an eagle soaring in the sky, and focus on yourself as a thing in motion. It will give you feelings of strength and grace that will help you keep going. The whole experience should be demanding but satisfying, not felt to be an awful chore. When you feel you want to stop, do. But be aware of *why* you have stopped. Are you short of breath? Anxious? Did you lose the image in motion? Your reasons will probably be different each time it happens.

Practise this for three weeks or so, allowing your pace and your images of motion to change according to how you feel each day. Sometimes you will go faster. Sometimes you will hold back. That is all part of the process. Simply be aware of what is happening and let it happen. Gradually you will find your body gaining strength, your breathing becoming easier and your movement more graceful. You will find that you are developing the art of being *here and now* in other areas of your life too. It gets easier and easier with practice. At the end of three weeks you will be bouncing with vitality and radiating a healthy glow. And your energy level – no matter what kind of energy you need, mental or physical – will have soared. That, after all, is what exercise for stress-wisdom is all about.

Eat Well

Today we return to food. You have given your system a good spring-clean in the past few days and are ready to start afresh with stress-wise eating. One of the things which most subjects your body to negative stress is eating the wrong kinds of food. The shelves of supermarkets and the tables in restaurants are full of tasty and seductive dishes which do little to strengthen your body's ability to handle stress positively yet use up a great deal of your precious adaptive energy. Most of these foods are made from refined flour and contain additives and preservatives. The typical packaged, ready-in-a-minute meal is high in hidden fats, food additives and sugars. They all put your body under stress.

Fat Chance for Freedom

Eating more fats than your body needs or eating the wrong kind of fats causes stress-damage. Too much fat prevents your body from making efficient use of carbohydrates and can encourage the development of diabetes. It raises fat and cholesterol levels in your blood as well as uric acid which contribute to the development of gout, arthritis and arteriosclerosis. A high-fat diet plays an important part in premature ageing and degenerative illnesses as well.

There are two kinds of fats, both of which you need to watch carefully if you want to be stress-wise: saturated and unsaturated. Saturated fats in milk products and meat are pretty useless except as a way of laying down more fat on your belly and hips. Eat a lot of saturated fats and you undermine health and leanness. The rest – unsaturated fats – are found in the processed oils you find on supermarket shelves gleaming all golden, or in margarines and convenience foods. Most have been chemically altered so your body cannot make use of the essential fatty acids they once contained. This can lead to fatty-acid deficiencies. Such deficiencies have now become widespread in the West despite our taking in almost half of the calories we eat in the form of fats.

When you eat a meal high in fat of *any* kind, the fat forms a film around your red blood platelets encouraging them to stick together. This clumping causes small capillaries to clog and even to shut down. As much as 20 per cent of your normal blood circulation can be lost, reducing the amount of oxygen available to your cells by about 30 per cent. This clumping and its corresponding oxygen-cell deficit lasts for many hours. In many people on the typical Western diet it is virtually continuous. The action of fat on the brain is one of the main reasons why you can feel sleepy or unable to think clearly after eating a heavy meal. Too much fat in your diet interferes with the high-level awareness and mental clarity that goes with handling stress well. You do not *need* to spread your bread with butter or pour lots of oils on your salads. A diet made up of at least 75 per cent vegetables, pulses, fruits and unrefined grains plus a few fresh seeds or nuts is the basis of stress-wise nutrition. Eaten with a little lean meat or fish if you like but without added oils, cheese or butter, it will give you all the fat you need to stay healthy – a mere 15 to 20 per cent of your daily calories. More than this subjects your body to unnecessary stress. Yet the average Westerner gets an amazing 45 per cent of their calories from fats – far too much for long-term health.

Don't Sugar Your Blood

Sugar also comes under the stress-wise axe. By now it is common knowledge that the consumption of refined sugar has been linked with the development of degenerative illnesses. Sugar, the end of a complex refining process which takes away every vitamin, mineral and trace of natural fibre from the beets or cane from which it is made, is a food virtually empty of nutritional benefit – except for calories. Eating sugar tends to raise your blood-sugar level and puts stress on your pancreas, challenging it to maintain normal blood-sugar levels. Sugar can also contribute to the development of arteriosclerosis. Yet most of us eat one kilogram or about two pounds a week of the stuff. In fact, about 20 to 25 per cent of our daily calories in the West come from it. Unless sugar is eaten naturally – that is the way you find it in a piece of fresh fruit – it is very hard on your body. It can make you tired, depressed and emotionally unstable due to the insulin resistance the raised blood-sugar level triggers in your body. It also leads to deficiencies in the B-complex vitamins and to an imbalance in important trace minerals.

Refined carbohydrates, such as white flour, white rice, and products made from them, are not much better. They don't put your body under stress as much as sugar and excess fats do, but they have been stripped of natural fibre important for detoxifying your body and protecting you from weight gain and the development of degenerative disease. Diabetes, coronary heart disease, dental caries, ulcers and even varicose veins have all been linked with an over-refined diet lacking in fibre, yet in our average Western fare, full of convenience foods, white bread and sugary goodies, nearly all the natural fibre has been removed. Put aside white bread and white pasta as well as anything containing white flour and you will automatically be protecting your body against a lot of unnecessary stress.

Junk the Coffee

One of the best things you can give up to improve your ability to handle stress is coffee. Just a few cups a day can both undermine your wellbeing and encourage you to age long before your time. Coffee contains caffeine and caffeine is a drug. One of the xanthine group of chemicals, it stimulates the central nervous system, pancreas and heart as well as the cerebral cortex – which is why, when you drink it, you feel temporarily more alert. Studies show, however, that while coffee drinking makes you think you are being more efficient, in reality it impedes your mental performance. Every time you drink a cup of coffee you are getting between 90 and 120 mg of caffeine. A cup of ordinary tea yields 40 to 100 mg, cocoa or cola drinks 20 to 50 mg. If you drink two to eight cups of coffee a day, you are getting a dose of the drug which any pharmacologist would reckon considerable. Taken day after day such a dose can be dangerous.

Caffeine can affect the heart, causing it to beat rapidly and irregularly. It increases the level of free fatty acids in your blood, stimulates the secretion of excess acid in the stomach and raises blood pressure. This raised blood-fat level is one of the suspected factors in arteriosclerosis, while secretion of excess acid in the stomach makes people more susceptible to gastric ulcers. Recent studies have also linked habitual coffee drinking to many stress disorders and certain mental illnesses – from quite simple depression and anxiety neurosis to overt psychosis. Caffeine, like the amphetamines which go into 'diet pills', can set off psychotic behaviour by acting on neuro-transmitters – chemicals in your brain which carry infor-mation across the tiny synapses between the nerve cells. The phenomenon of caffeine producing mental and emotional aberrations is termed 'caffeinism'. Also inter-esting is caffeine's effect on the body when you stop drinking coffee. For coffee, if you are a steady 'user', is addictive. Its removal can cause powerful withdrawal symptoms. These usually appear as nausea or a headache which lasts from a few hours to several days, depending on how serious the addiction and how finely tuned your system is. But the withdrawal symptoms are short-lived and worth going through to be rid of caffeine once and for all.

Go Light on Protein

The idea that you need to eat meat to stay healthy is also untrue. Studies show that a mixed diet of roots, grains, vegetables and fruits is a much better source of high-quality protein than are the traditional meat, fish and dairy products which are high in fat and too concen-trated in protein. Eat meat, fish and game by all means if you want but in small quantities, say 85–112 grams or three or four ounces a day, instead of as the main food in a meal. Or eat them only occasionally. Try to make sure it is *really* lean meat too, like venison for instance or wild boar. And remember that the vegetables you eat contain a good quantity of protein, as do pulses. Eat them together with your grains for high-grade protection. A bowl of chilli beans eaten with a piece of corn bread will give you the full complement of all the essential amino-acids without the excess of fat. You don't need to eat flesh foods at all if you prefer.

Until recently our need for protein has been grossly exaggerated. Most of us in the West get far more than we need. Your body needs the constituents of protein – amino-acids – to build muscle, make new hormones and carry out its metabolic processes, such as growth and the repair and maintenance of bodily tissue. But when it gets too much protein this leaches precious minerals and trace elements, such as zinc, calcium, magnesium, iron and chromium, from bones and tissues. These minerals are not only essential to your health, the maintenance of firm skin and shining hair, but to your emotional well-being. A high-protein diet, especially a diet high in meat, has been shown to play a leading role in the genesis of osteoporosis and arteriosclerosis. No more than 15 to 20 per cent of your calorie intake needs to come from protein foods.

Carbs are King

Another common assumption which a stress-wise way of eating challenges is the idea that you mustn't eat too many carbohydrates because 'starches are not really good for you'. Carbohydrates are the best thing you can eat for physical and emotional balance, provided, of course, they are complex carbohydrates – unrefined grains, pulses, vegetables and fruits eaten in as natural a state as possible. Starches such as brown rice or wheat which have not been milled to death and deprived of most of their natural vitamins, minerals and fibre, when taken together with fresh vegetables, provide a steady stream of energy. What's so special about vegetables? Plenty. They have powerful health-enhancing properties which is why diets high in fresh vegetables are recommended as protection against degenerative diseases such as cancer, arthritis and arteriosclerosis. Important, too, is making sure that a good proportion of your vegetables is eaten raw. This can increase the micro-electric potential of your body's tissues, making cells function better, improving intra- and extra-cellular exchange and imparting high levels of mental and physical vitality. Fresh vegetables are also a rich source of natural fibre, vitamins and minerals. Unlike sugar and over-refined foods these complex carbohydrates will never over-stimulate the pancreas or encourage the development of unstable blood-sugar levels, obesity or diabetes. But they can heighten your resistance to illness. Meanwhile, eating grains affects the chemistry of the brain by enhancing the production of serotonin, which helps you keep your cool when all around you people are losing theirs.

STRESS-WISE EATING	STRESS-FOOLISH FOODS
Fresh vegetables and fruits	Refined sugar and flour and products made from them
Fresh vegetable juices	Highly processed foods and ready-made meals
Natural unsweetened low-fat yoghurt – especially goat's milk yoghurt	Preservatives, additives, artificial flavouring, colouring, stabilizers, emulsifiers, etc.
Fermented foods – natural sauerkraut (for instance)	Alcohol, coffee
Wholegrain breads, pasta and cereals	Excess fat, excess protein
Beans and lentils	Most ready-made packaged cereals
Green foods like spirulina, chlorella, green barley, alfalfa and seaweeds	Squashes, colas, diet sodas and drinks

Treasures from the Sea

Seaweeds can be helpful in enhancing your body's ability to handle stress. All seaweeds – from kelp and dulse to the Japanese nori and kombu – are rich in the minerals which your body's metabolic processes require to function properly. Since convenience foods are greatly depleted in minerals and trace elements, the use of plants from the sea becomes more and more important. Even things which your system requires in minute quantities such as vanadium, chromium and lithium can be found in sea plants. Sea plants also tend to be rich in special forms of fibre called alginates which have the ability to bind and remove toxic heavy metals from the body. And they are rich in organic iodine. A good supplement of sea plants which have been collected from unpolluted waters and then 'atomized' or broken into very fine particles can offer another source of important metabolic support on any anti-stress diet. Keep up the green drinks too. They are alkalinizing to the body and help counteract the acidity associated with stress.

A Stress-wise Diet

A stress-wise diet contains no more than 15 to 20 per cent of its calories in the form of fat, and no more than 15 to 20 per cent in the form of protein. It is made up of complex carbohydrates including fresh cooked or raw fruits, vegetables, pulses, grains and very small amounts of low-fat dairy products, plus a little meat, fish or fowl if you want it. It excludes sugar, convenience foods and refined carbohydrates such as white rice, white bread, sweets and pasta made from white flour. It also excludes coffee and includes only small amounts of alcohol.

Such a diet is quite naturally low in calories. Thanks to

97

TYPICAL WESTERN DIET (calories %)	**STRESS-WISE EATING** (calories %)
25–35% carbohydrate (simple)	60–75% carbohydrate (complex)
25% protein	15–20% protein
40–50% fat	15–20% fat

its low fat content it allows you to eat as much as you like without gaining weight. Unlike sugar, refined cereals and breads, the unrefined grains, fruits and vegetables are slowly digested and assimilated. They provide your body with continuous energy throughout the day, eliminating blood-sugar problems and helping you avoid fatigue. Overweight people who have been put on this kind of diet find themselves losing weight without consciously restricting their calorie intake, and feeling far more energetic. The reason for this is simple: they have eliminated all the unnecessary 'stressors' from their diet and emphasized the life supporters – natural, unrefined foods which contain the highest complement of nutrients vital to life. The stress-wise approach to nutrition may at first seem a very different way of eating from what you are used to – eliminating the sweets, white flour and large quantities of meat and gravy. If you are in the habit of putting lots of butter on your foods, it seems strange at first to eat so little of it. But it is fairly simple to learn to cook foods without lots of fats as well as eliminating sugary foods and refined flour. And if you make the changes slowly week by week you will soon get used to pulses and grains. Whether you embrace the whole anti-stress way of eating or simply adjust your usual way of eating to bring it more in line with the stress-wise dietetic principles, within only a few weeks you will discover that you are on to something good. Try it and see.

A Typical Day on the Stress-wise Diet

On rising

A cup of hot water to which the juice of half a lemon has been added to help alkalinize your system and promote good elimination

Breakfast

An orange or half a grapefruit. A bowl of homemade low-fat yoghurt

or

A bowl of porridge made from steel-cut whole oats, with sliced banana and cinnamon on top, and skimmed milk

or

Bircher Muesli made with low-fat yoghurt

Herb tea (or coffee substitute)

Mid-morning, if desired

Green drink (see Day Two)

or

A piece of raw fruit

or

Some sticks of raw vegetables such as carrots or celery

or

A slice of wholegrain bread on its own or spread with non-fat cottage cheese and sprinkled with red pepper

Lunch

A bowl of homemade vegetable or lentil soup, made without fat

A large salad made from raw vegetables such as lettuce, chicory, watercress, green and red peppers, celery, cauliflower, peas, sprouted seeds or grains, with a non-oil salad dressing such as a yoghurt dressing, or sprinkled with lemon juice

99

STRESS-WISE NUTRITION	WHAT TO EAT	WHAT NOT TO EAT
Meat, fish, game and poultry	Chicken and turkey, preferably without the skin which is too fat. Very lean wild fish, game, meat or offal cooked without fat (no more than 112 g or 4 oz three or four times a week)	Ham, sausages, bacon, smoked meats, farmed salmon, tinned tuna
Grains, breads and cereals	All wholegrains such as brown rice, rye, millet, wholewheat, rolled oats, breads, wholewheat pasta, wholegrain pitta bread, Essene bread, crispbreads	Bread or pastry products or cereals made with sugar or bleached white flour, soya flour (too much protein), white biscuits and scones. Processed foods
Pulses	All beans, peas and lentils	
Fats and oils	Very little, except what occurs naturally in the grains, seeds, nuts, vegetables and fruits, plus small quantities of butter and cold-pressed virgin olive oil	

STRESS-WISE NUTRITION	WHAT TO EAT	WHAT NOT TO EAT
Fruits and vegetables	All fruits (but no more than five portions a day), all vegetables (unlimited amounts) eaten raw, steamed or lightly cooked in a little oil in a wok or baked and cooked without fat	
Dairy products	Cheese made from skimmed milk, yoghurt made from skimmed milk (not more than 56 g or 2oz a day)	Whole milk and cream, most cheeses (too fat and chemically fermented), tinned milk
Sweets, drinks and spices	Fresh fruit, dandelion coffee or coffee substitutes, herb teas, vinegar, fresh or dried herbs, spices, cayenne pepper	Coffee, tea, sugar, sugared drinks, sugar-free soft drinks, chocolate or anything containing sugar, salty savouries such as crisps, rich or heavy sauces

Mid-afternoon, if desired
Same as mid-morning

Dinner
A 112 g or 4 oz piece of chicken roasted without the skin
(the skin contains lots of fat)
or
A 112 g or 4 oz piece of poached fish served without
sauce but with a wedge of lemon
As many steamed vegetables without butter or sauce as
you like, such as spinach, broccoli, cauliflower, Brussels
sprouts, carrots
A bowl of steamed brown rice
A green salad with 1 tablespoon olive oil and lemon
dressing (or try low-fat yoghurt and crushed fresh
herbs)
A wholegrain roll or two without butter
A glass of wine, if desired
Fresh fruit

What About Supplementary Vitamins and Minerals?

Controversy rages over whether or not you need to take
supplementary vitamins and minerals if you are following
a good dietary lifestyle such as the stress-wise one. If you
do not live in a city and you eat most of your foods out of
your own garden where they have been organically grown,
you probably don't. If not, many experts in nutrition
insist it is a wise thing to do. But how do you choose a
formula? By carefully reading labels and by knowing what
you are looking for. Basically there are two ways to go
when it comes to food supplements – the conservative
'guard against any possible deficiencies' and the more

STRESS-WISE SUPPLEMENTS	LOW-TECH	HIGH-TECH
Vitamin A	5000 IU	25000 IU
Vitamin B1	25 mg	100 mg
Vitamin B2	25 mg	100 mg
Vitamin B3	50 mg	100 mg
Vitamin B5	40 mg	100 mg
Vitamin B6	40 mg	100 mg
Vitamin B12	40 mcg	100 mcg
Folic Acid	200 mcg	400 mcg
Biotin	100 mcg	500 mcg
Choline	100 mg	100 mg
Inositol	100 mg	100 mg
PABA	50 mg	100 mg
Vitamin C	500 mg	2000–10000 mg
Bioflavonoids	50 mg	200 mg
Vitamin D	300 IU	400 IU
Vitamin E	100 IU	200–1200 IU
Calcium	100 mg	500–1000 mg
Magnesium	50 mg	250–500 mg
Potassium	10 mg	50 mg
Iron	10 mg	25 mg
Copper	1 mg	1 mg
Zinc	10 mg	35 mg
Manganese	2 mg	10 mg
Molybdenum	50 mcg	75 mcg
Chromium	25 mcg	200 mcg
Selenium	25 mcg	200 mcg
Iodine	75 mcg	150 mcg
Boron	1 mcg	2 mcg

avant-garde mega-nutrient approach which is based on the notion that nutritional supplements should be used to counter pollution, protect against ageing, and the belief that in larger quantities they may be able to increase energy levels and even promote a higher level of health. What you find below is in no way intended to be prescriptive. Each person is unique. Your own requirements need to be worked out with the help of a physician knowledgeable about nutrition or a qualified nutritionist. If you decide to take supplements, you will probably find the ones you choose will lie somewhere between the two extremes. The conservative approach is the column on the left, the mega-nutrient approach you will find in the right-hand column.

The most important thing of all to remember is that stress-wise eating is first and foremost based on *food* not nutritional supplements. Eat this way and you get maximum protection against stress-damage not only right now but in all the years to come.

Get Clear

Just as you need to move your body to become stress-hardy, you also need to make full use of the remarkable powers of your mind – the *whole* of your mind which includes both the right and left hemisphere of your brain. For subtle shifts in the way you think – the way you perceive the world around you – more than anything else can help free you from the ravages of stress. To make such shifts one needs to take the relaxation response a step further into the realm of expanding consciousness. That is what Day Seven of the *10 Day Destress Plan* asks you to consider.

Meet Our Worldview

Mind and body, far from being two separate entities are really opposite ends of a *bodymind* continuum – two aspects of the same living being which is you. The notion of bodymind as a single entity may seem strange to you. For we have grown up in a materialistic culture that has long ignored mental and spiritual influences in its attempt to reduce the phenomenon of life to mere random chemical and physical events. All this has developed out of

105

our rather limited *worldview.* A worldview is a way of look-ing at the world which remains unconscious in a culture but which tends to govern the judgements we all make as part of that culture. It is a kind of unspoken consensus about reality. Our materialistic and fragmented worldview contributes greatly to the widespread stress that is so much a part of our culture. It is etched deep into the fabric of the unconscious assumptions that govern how we live our lives. Until the seventeenth century the unity of mind and body formed an integral part of people's world-view as well as the belief systems and healing practices that grew out of it, which had existed as far back as ancient Egypt or even before. Ayurvedic medicine – the oldest known system of healing in the world – is based on such a unity. So is Chinese medicine and spiritual healing. But in eighteenth-century Europe, after the onset of the Industrial Revolution and following in the wake of Descartes and Newton, the unified worldview changed as the intellect became king, and such ways of perceiving as instinct and intuition were banished to the dungeon of outmoded ideas. Yet intellect is only part of the way the human brain functions.

Personal and Planetary Disasters

Reason and intellect are activities of the left hemisphere of the brain. Your brain's right hemisphere works quite differently – not by seeing the world in fragments but by looking at things intuitively in their wholeness and experiencing the inter-relationship of all the parts. When, in the eighteenth century, we in the West began to ignore intuition and to glorify reason, we started to see all phenomena in the universe, even life itself, as nothing more than a collection of complex yet ultimately explain-able, random chemical and physical events. We came to believe that the whole is nothing more than the sum of these parts and we came to look upon ourselves as quite separate from the world around us. We also created an educational system which places exclusive emphasis on developing left-brain skills and neglects the development of the right.

Not only has our over-emphasis on left-brain reason led us to exploit the resources of our planet without regard for the consequences of our actions, it has also wreaked havoc with our lives. It has created for many an experience of continuous stress very much akin to being a fish out of water. For an exclusively left-brain worldview brings in its wake a sense of meaninglessness – viewing all of life the way it does as fragmented. Far from making us feel safe or nurtured as part of all life, it tends to produce anxiety in us and a sense of helplessness. When both right and left hemispheres of the brain are equally developed, however, then much of the existential angst that underlies chronic stress disappears.

Marriage of Right and Left

One of life's deepest and most constant stresses for any of us is trying to live from the intellect alone. Doing so creates experience of life where the person living it feels they have continually to hang on to all the pieces of their life lest it fall apart. It also brings about a sense of purposelessness since all of the events in one's life and all of the choices that one makes appear to be entirely arbitrary. Yet few people realize that our experience of contemporary angst is the result of too limited a worldview and is a by-product of the way we have been educated – trained to rely too much on our intellect while the development of our instinctive, creative, right-hemisphere skills have been largely ignored. That is the bad news. The good news is that it is never too late to change things for the better. Recent research into brain activity, brain-wave patterns, and their relationship to thoughts, events and experiences has demonstrated that the mind has enormous potential for expansion. Your brain develops depending upon how it is used. When the left hemisphere has been over-developed and the right hemisphere under-developed there are many neurological links that have simply not yet been made. What is exciting is that the regular practice of a deep relaxation or meditation technique appears to help make new connections between different areas of the brain. Not only does your thinking become more efficient, you also gain a much better balance between intellect and intuition. As this happens you begin to experience reality in a much more complete and satisfying way. And you can use simple pleasant methods to help bring this about.

Mindspans

There are two aspects of deep relaxation or meditation that are particularly important for triggering the relaxation response. The first is the *constant repetition* of a sound, a prayer or a physical action. This effectively silences the stressful 'brain chatter' most of us live with day in day out. The second is a *passive attitude* where you mentally observe what is happening. Such a passive attitude evokes right-brain activity. You simply observe without defining what you are seeing or acting on any of your thoughts the way a young child might. Herbert Benson has done a great deal of work with the expansion of consciousness in this way. He calls it developing *maximum mind*. He and others have found that invoking the relaxation response opens a door to expanding the brain and mind both neurologically in making new connections and in terms of the way a person views reality. When you regularly practise a method of meditation or a technique which does this, an inner awareness grows that each of us has an enormous capacity to change our life in whatever way we may want it changed. With this realization comes a growing sense of personal power and confidence. For invoking the relaxation response again and again enhances communications between right and left hemispheres. It also increases the coherence of certain brain-wave frequencies – alpha and beta in particular – in both the right and the left hemispheres, enabling the brain to work better as a whole.

Learning New Skills

The right brain works in a very different way from the left. Your left brain is critical, focused and rational. It can only deal with one thing at a time. Your right hemisphere knows no such barriers. Psychologists and other researchers who have examined our unconscious processes – with which the right hemisphere of the brain is closely linked – discovered that the unconscious has no space/time limits. It does not separate what it experiences as happening now with what it experienced from earlier times nor even from what may come in the future. This is an experience which is anathema to your rational left brain but one which your right brain grasps with ease. The right hemisphere with its close association with the unconscious does not differentiate between a *real* event and an imagined one. This timelessness, sense of wholeness, and inability to differentiate between what is imaginary and what is real makes the right brain and the unconscious useful in expanding your consciousness.

Unlike the left brain which measures every thought with which you present it against external reality, the right brain tends to measure what it is offered by the *intensity* of an image or an experience evoked. How vivid is it? How much emotive power does it carry? How well does it free the imagination? These are the criteria your unconscious uses in deciding to move into action or not. And when the right brain is allowed to play upon an intense image often enough it can bring what it is imaging into being. This is where advanced stages of the relaxation response come into their own. For when you have practised inducing it regularly for some time and new brain connections are forged, you can begin to make use of this state to re-programme your life.

Here's how. Allowing your mind to focus on some positive idea – it could be a passage from a book that you are very drawn to, or a happy photograph or painting – sit in a state of deep relaxation and simply read over the passage or look at the picture for five to ten minutes, allowing yourself very gently to sit with what is before you. Alternatively, pick up a piece of paper and a pencil and write a passage yourself, letting the words simply flow out of you, words about a hope that you have perhaps, or a dream, or what is of greatest value to you in your life. Let your mind play upon your word-making as a child might sit in the middle of the floor playing with a toy. When doing this you don't need to concentrate or try to change yourself in any way. In fact if you do try you actually undermine the ability of whatever you are looking at, reading, writing or in the presence of, to further unify your brain. Instead give your right hemisphere complete freedom to operate and interact with the left, opening the door to the possibility that what you dream, what you believe in, can in time be lived fully and truly in your own life.

Bodymind Defined

When the brain becomes better balanced in its functions you feel more at peace. This has a positive effect on your whole body. For generations a few have preached the power of mind to influence body. Only recently, however, have researchers begun to draw scientific maps of *how* this happens. Most of the new knowledge comes out of a fascinating medical and biochemical discipline with an absurdly long name: *psychoneuroimmunology* or PNI.

PNI is the scientific study of bodymind. Leading researchers in the PNI field, such as Dr G. F. Solomon at the University of California, have discovered that the human mind (which includes our conscious thoughts and unconscious impulses as well as our *superconscious* or transcendent mind and our emotions) is elaborately interwoven with every function of the body via nerve pathways and chemical messengers – endorphins, neuropeptides and hormones. A hormonal–nerve relationship exists between your endocrine glands, via the pituitary (master gland regulating the actions of all others), the adrenals (which deal with stress) and the hypothalamus. It is called the hypo-thalamic-pituitary-adrenal-axis and it links your thoughts and emotions with physical responses. New evidence even suggests that, rather like a physicist's electrons which appear as either waves or particles depending upon expectations, your body's chemical messengers – the neuropeptides – may be made up of a single molecule whose configuration can be altered by your mental, emotional and spiritual state to create new forms. With each passing month more scientific maps of bodymind are being drawn. They show how what you think and feel powerfully influence the levels of vitality you experience, as well as how slowly or rapidly you age, and whether or not you resist infections.

111

To make a quantum leap in becoming stress-hardy –
not to mention to prevent the kind of environmental
destruction which could well eliminate the human race –
each of us needs to expand our vision of reality. We need
to develop a new, broader and more appropriate worldview – one which helps unify right and left hemispheres
of the brain as well as mind and body. Such vision takes
time to evolve, but it happens quite naturally, gradually
becoming incorporated into our unconscious. Then,
instead of *limiting* our ability to care for ourselves in optimum ways, it empowers us to do so.

For many who have worked long-term with the relaxation response in this way it has resulted in the development of a new worldview which encompasses
important concepts which only a few years ago would
have seemed absurdities to the average person and
may still do to some. Such a new worldview usually also
includes a growing sense that somewhere deep within
is a way of *knowing* beyond the limits of our conscious
awareness. There is much evidence that, provided we
are willing to open ourselves to that knowing and to
look beneath the surface of everyday reality, we are
each capable of discovering new solutions to old problems. We are also able to release blocked creativity and
achieve levels of physical and emotional wellbeing that
before have seemed far beyond our reach in the stress-
filled and polluted environment in which most of us
now live.

It is very much like making a new friend when you
begin to tap into the power for change which emerges as
you use more and more of your brain. Once you come to
respect this process and learn how it works, you can
begin to draw on its almost infinite power for healing,
transformation, problem-solving and – best of all – for
creativity. By creativity I not only mean being able to

112

write or paint, or arrange flowers or play music, but being able to create the life you want to live and live it.

Let Yourself Play

How you use the deeply relaxed state to expand your mind is really up to you. You might choose simply to look at something happy or listen to a beautiful piece of music which in time enhances your own capacity for joy. What you are calling forth are the powers of active imagination through contemplation of something – words, sound, images, thoughts or dreams. The more often you repeat the process the deeper the beneficial effect it can have on your mind. You can also use it as a way of defining your personal belief system and discovering what has meaning in your life or as a way of planting seeds for whatever it is you want to create in the future. There are two important keys: first that you regularly use some technique for deep relaxation or meditation to put your mind into a fully relaxed state and, secondly, that you let yourself simply enjoy the interaction with whatever thoughts, dreams or pleasures you have chosen to interact with.

Quantum Mind

What is remarkable about practising this more advanced stage of contemplative thought, is that after you have done so for even a couple of weeks you notice subtle but important shifts taking place in the way you think and act. You discover you are looking upon life more positively. What I find tremendously exciting, although I don't claim to understand fully how it happens, is that many of the conflicts which once caused continual stress seem to dissipate, or you find new ways of handling them

113

effectively. Some psychologists and spiritual teachers working with the active imagination in these ways believe that it brings access to the vast unconscious mind within each of us, which has the capacity to transform both the way our bodies function and the overall quality of our whole life regardless of external circumstances.

In recent years the capacity of active imagination has been much used by forward-thinking sports coaches. To improve performance they get their athletes to sit or lie down, shut their eyes and day-dream, imagining them-selves, say, clearing the high-jump set higher than ever before. It has also been used with biofeedback training in teaching people to evoke the help of their unconscious mind to alter blood pressure that is too high or dissi-pate an agonizing migraine by imagining their hands growing warm, thus drawing congested blood out of the head and ameliorating the pain. Making use of this superb imaginative power asks that you provide your unconscious with vibrant images of what you want to create or experience – images it loves to play on whether these be words or visual pictures or even vague longings. Whatever they are these need to be images you find excit-ing, pleasing, fun. It also asks that you allow your mind to play with these images while in a deeply relaxed state over and over again.

Using repetition and evocative words, images and thoughts in this way, your unconscious mind's ability to alter your life for the better appears almost unlimited. The unconscious can enable us, if we so choose, to clear out false beliefs and ancient emotional shadows. It can help us change what we want to change, heal what we want to heal and even create things which for years we have been longing to create but against all hope. So effective is this kind of imaginative right-brain play that not to work with these simple yet powerful techniques which spur your unconscious into action is like trying to live your life with one hand tied behind your back. Choose one or two things which appeal to you, such as a picture or poem, and in a state of deep relaxation let your mind play with it for five minutes or so each day. It can not only help release you from much chronic stress; it can teach your spirit how to soar.

Day Eight

Earth Works

Let's look at herbs on Day Eight. The right kind of herbs can be a great asset not only during times of heavy pressure but also to help increase your body's adaptive energy, so you can take a lot more pressure without cracking. Hans Selye, the father of stress, did not believe this could be done. Now, thanks mostly to research carried out in Russia, we know it can – provided you know your herbs well and choose the right ones.

There are two classes of herbs that are helpful en route to becoming stress-hardy. The first are the adaptogens. These are agents which can help protect you against mental and physical fatigue and offer non-specific resistance against stress, as well as an ability to balance or normalize either excessive or deficient physiological functions in your body. The second group are the problem-solvers such as valerian – an excellent alternative to tranquillizers when you need some extra help – or echinacea, which is an immune booster should you feel yourself in danger of getting a cold or 'flu during very demanding periods.

Let the Buyer Beware

The sale of herbals in Europe alone is approaching a thousand million pounds a year. Disillusionment with synthetic drugs has led even the medical profession to take a new look at the great promise which herbal medicine holds for the future. Everyone seems to be on the herbal bandwagon. But beware. All that glitters is not gold. Many herbs on the market are either contaminated with pesticides, have been grown on depleted soils using artificial fertilizers or have been irradiated. All three practices not only reduce the effectiveness of herbal products by decreasing active substances in them or rendering these substances not available to the body, they can actually result in negative effects, including poisoning. Similarly, much of the information about herbs and how to use them in the popular press is anecdotal, often inaccurate and sometimes totally misleading. There seems to be an unspoken assumption that just because something is 'natural' it is bound to be good for you. Nothing could be further from the truth. You need to know your herbs before you ever consider using them as nutritional supplements. You also need to know your source and to be sure that the herbs you take are not irradiated. Look for those which have been grown on organic soils to preserve the trace elements and the chemical content of the plant, are fresh, and have been skilfully handled to preserve their health-enhancing properties. Most herbs are sensitive to light and oxygen.

Although herbalists frequently use extracts and tinctures, most often the best way to take any herb yourself is *whole* in powdered form – in a capsule if you want to avoid any unpleasant taste. There is a certain magic in a whole herb simply because in its wholeness you find remarkable synergy – a synergy to which the living body is highly receptive. For instance, the herb valerian contains compounds such as *valtrate* and *didrovaltrate* which were long believed to be its active principles offering a sedative effect. New research shows that other chemicals in the plant such as the *alpha-ethylpyrrol ketone* may be equally important. Rather like people, each herb has its own personality. Get to know them, they can be great friends for stress and overall health, enhancing your energy levels, protecting you from fatigue and illness, and helping you to unwind. Let's look at the adaptogens first.

Medicines for the Well

The adaptogens, which include a wide variety of natural substances from Panax ginseng and eleuthrococcus (sometimes called Siberian ginseng) to an exotic-sounding preparation made from the horn of a deer, have been widely investigated in recent years by Soviet scientists, and in centuries past by the Orientals. Most adaptogens belong to a long tradition of folk medicine and most have been held in high esteem for thousands of years in the pharmacopoeia of the world's medicine. What is special about these natural products, and the reason why they are grouped together under the name adaptogen, is that carefully conducted laboratory and clinical studies have shown that each is capable of enhancing an organism's 'non-specific resistance' to ageing, illness and fatigue. In practical terms they improve your ability to adapt to all forms of stress, while at the same time helping to normalize its biochemical effects. Taken as 'medicines for well people' adaptogens can be remarkably helpful in keeping you youthful and full of vitality. They have been shown to increase physical stamina and endurance, stimulate protein repair on a cellular level, protect from radiation damage, increase antibody produc-

118

tion, detoxify your body and improve stamina and vitality. In a way the adaptogens could be considered the natural 'elixirs of life'.

Soviet scientists first developed the notion of an adaptogen from the work of Hans Selye. Selye was always fascinated with the idea that it might be possible to discover or to develop 'medicines for well people' which could enhance our body's own adaptation mechanisms and which could prolong our ability to resist age-degeneration and exhaustion. They would have to be different from usual medicines in that, unlike drugs, they would not be aimed at a specific effect such as lowering blood pressure or eliminating pain. Nor would they be intended for the treatment of illness. They would belong to a new category of medicines for health which would improve the body's *non-specific resistance* to illness, ageing and fatigue. That's where the adaptogens come in – substances which can increase your general capacity to overcome external stresses through adaptation.

Russian researcher I. I. Brekhman at the Institute of Marine Biology Far-East Scientific Centre of the Academy of Science in Vladivostock has probably done more than any other single scientist to find natural substances with adaptogenic properties and to test their effects both on animals and humans. In fact it was Brekhman's teacher, the Russian expert in pharmacology, N.V. Lazarev, who first coined the word 'adaptogen' in order to describe these substances with the remarkable ability to strengthen and re-balance the whole system. One of the first natural substances which Brekhman and his co-workers investigated which had this ability was Panax ginseng. Probably the most well-known and highly respected natural medicine in the world, the ginseng root was first used for medicinal purposes more than 4,000 years ago 'to restore the five internal organs, tranquillize the spirit, calm agitation of the mind, allay excitement, and ward off harmful influences.'

For Perfect Harmony

Traditionally ginseng has been prescribed only in states of imbalance. It is used to treat toxicity in the body, sluggishness, anaemia, weakness and fatigue. On a perfectly healthy and balanced person it was once believed to have no effect whatever. For a long time in the West ginseng was dismissed as an old wives' tale – in part because the very notion of a medicine for health finds little room in the thinking behind Western orthodox medicine, and in part because some of the studies in the West which were carried out to test the root's properties had been done on inferior crops or on ginseng which had been carelessly processed. Over-processing and heat treatments destroy many of the beneficial effects of the adaptogens. As a result most of the ginsengs you find on the market are pretty useless. You need to choose your products carefully.

There are three true ginseng plants. Panax ginseng is the original Korean/Chinese plant; Tienchi (Panax noto-ginseng) is another Eastern version of the plant; and Panax Quinquefolius, or American ginseng. The active chemicals in ginseng are compounds called ginsenosides of which there are thirteen. These fatty compounds of hydrogen and oxygen, which are derived from essential oils, lie at the core of ginseng's anti-stress properties. They are the active ingredients. When choosing ginseng you need to look for a standardized ginseng extract with a guaranteed percentage of ginsenosides – for instance, the Swiss standardized ginseng extract G115. Panax ginseng comes from Korea or China. The best-quality roots are the big red ones which are six years old. Next best are the white roots and third are the red roots grown in Japan, so look for the country of origin when buying them and also for the Korean 'Office of Monopoly' seal on the pack. The whole roots are best to take, with root pieces and extracts following in that order. There is also one excellent ginseng tea (see Resources). Ginseng tablets and powders often contain 'fillers' and are much less potent. American ginseng – Panax Quinquefolius – is usually less effective than Panax ginseng, unless you can get large old roots which are hard to come by.

Perfect Stimulant

Thanks to a number of well-conducted studies – on both animals and humans – carried out by Brekhman and others in the Soviet Union and by European researchers in Switzerland, Sweden, Germany and Britain, we now know that ginseng has powerful adaptogenic properties. It improves your body's ability to use oxygen, increases mental stamina and improves athletic performance. It helps to lower blood pressure that is too high, although it doesn't affect normal readings. It increases your resistance to illness and to the harmful effects of chemicals in the environment and is a natural stimulant to the central nervous system – improving reflexes, long-term and short-term memory, and making learning easier. Unlike coffee, and most other stimulants in common use, ginseng does not produce a sudden rapid rise in blood sugar followed by an unpleasant dip in energy. Nor is there any danger of becoming dependent on it, for it has the remarkable ability to harmonize the body's biochemistry. Ginseng is a particular boon to athletes under physical stress because it also has been shown to reduce lactic acid levels. In an interesting double-blind study carried out for twelve weeks in Australia on experienced athletes, researchers discovered that ginseng was able to increase muscle strength significantly – 22 per cent in the case of the pectorals and 18 per cent in quadriceps strength – as well as to reduce recovery time from exhaustive exercise. At the University of Minnesota, researchers tested the exam-taking abilities of students by giving some of them ginseng and others a placebo: the exam results from the ginseng group were significantly better than the placebo-takers. Also, in repeated animal trials, Brekhman and others have found that ginseng acts as a stimulant without causing insomnia, and that it not only helps stave off fatigue but also strengthens the organism as a whole.

The beneficial effects of taking ginseng multiply and build up over the period in which it is used. And ginseng's benefits last long after you stop taking it. As Brekhman says:

> After a series of experiments on men it was established that daily doses of ginseng preparations during fifteen to forty-five days increase physical endurance and mental capacity for work. The increase was noted not only during the treatment itself, but also for a month to a month and a half after the treatment finished. The increase in work capacity was attended by a number of favourable somatic effects and a general improvement of health and spirits (appetite, sleep, absence of moodiness).

Siberian Ginseng

Another adaptogen which has now been widely investigated, particularly in the Soviet Union, is *Eleuthrococcus senticosus* or Siberian ginseng. A member of the same family but really a different species, eleuthrococcus had not been used by many generations: its therapeutic properties were only discovered in the past 50 years. Siberian ginseng is a prickly plant known as 'devil's shrub' with leaves similar to ginseng and beautiful yellow and purple flowers. It is the plant's hot and spicy roots which are used medicinally. Like ginseng, it has the capacity to strengthen the body's ability to resist illness, degeneration and fatigue, while never upsetting its natural physiological functions. It is also a mild stimulant, the stimulant action lasting between six and eight hours. But its tonic effects are cumulative – they come gradually over a few weeks. They include increased stamina, better sleep patterns, better memory, clearer thinking and improved athletic performance.

Brekhman and many Russian researchers believe that eleuthrococcus is an even better adaptogen than ginseng. And it is considered by Russian physicians to be a treatment of choice for both high and low blood pressure thanks again to its ability to harmonize bodily functions with no side effects. But there have so far been very few well-controlled studies to validate their claims. Like ginseng and all of the adaptogens, it is best taken regularly over a period of several weeks. It can, however, be taken year-round without any loss in beneficial effects. The best form of *Eleuthrococcus senticosus* comes in extract direct from the Soviet Union. It has been carefully low-heat processed to preserve its biological activity. This kind of extract is used in some of the German Siberian ginseng preparations.

Amazon Power

The most exciting herb I have come across for a long time is suma (*Pfaffia paniculata*). Locally known as Para Todo – 'for everything' – suma has been used by Brazilian Indians for centuries as an aphrodisiac and general tonic. Recent research shows that, like good ginseng, the wild root of the suma plant also has strong adaptogenic properties. Amongst its other constituents, suma is rich in the saponins, some of which show anti-tumour activity, and in a plant hormone called *ecdysone*. At the University of São Paulo, Dr Milton Brazzach, Chairman of Pharmacology, has treated thousands of patients with serious ailments, including both diabetes and cancer, and verified the plant's potent healing and preventative powers. Researchers have found that a major source of the plant's energy-enhancing and stress-protective properties lies in its ability to detoxify connective tissue of what are called *homotoxins*. These are wastes which can interfere with the active transport of nutrients to the cells and in the production of cellular energy, and lead long-term to changes in the DNA associated with premature ageing and the development of degenerative diseases. What all of this means to the active man or woman is that suma is well worth looking at as a nutritional support to raise your energy levels, enhance your ability to be very active both mentally and physically without fatigue or damage, and to detoxify your cells as a prevention against premature ageing and degeneration.

Daisy with a Difference

Apart from the adaptogenics which strengthen the organism against stress, there are two general herbs which can be a real help during times of heavy pressure – echinacea and valerian.

The immune system plays an important part in protecting from stress-damage. For prolonged stress increases the cortical steroid and catecholamine hormones which leads to an immuno-suppressive state and means that you can become highly susceptible to infectious illnesses. That's where echinacea comes in handy. Known as Purple

Coneflower, echinacea is a member of the Compositae (daisy) family with potent antibiotic and anti-viral effects. The roots of two species, *E. purpurea* and *E. angustifolia*, have long been used against infection and in detoxifying the body by native peoples including the American Plains' Indians, who also used it for poisonous snake and spider bites, abscesses, diphtheria, measles, chicken pox, septic wounds and many other infectious or immune-compromising conditions.

In recent years the herb has been heavily researched in Germany where numerous scientific studies now verify its health-promoting abilities. In Germany there are now more than 200 prescription products based on echinacea or its derivatives. The herb can inhibit the growth of viruses and bacteria that cause colds and 'flu, increase the number of valuable B-cells in the body and enhance the protective functions of macrophages – white blood cells which are guardians of the immune system. In short, echinacea is able to amplify the activity of the immune system not only by helping an ailing body to recover swiftly, but by helping protect from infections such as colds and 'flu during the long winter months.

I find particularly interesting some recent research in the treatment of vaginal thrush where the herb was used. All the women in the study were treated with conventional anti-fungal drug agents. Some were also given echinacea – the equivalent of 1000–2000 mg a day. As any woman who has ever suffered from it knows only too well, one of the major problems with thrush is although you can knock it out, it tends to recur especially when you are under stress. Researchers discovered that amongst the echinacea-supplemented group there was a significantly lower recurrence of infection than amongst the rest. And the protection went far beyond thrush. They also found a heightened immune response to tetanus, diphtheria, streptococci and tuberculin. What is exciting about their findings is that they concluded that, unlike antibiotic drugs, echinacea does not attack germs directly. Instead it strengthens your body's own ability to resist them and heightens your defences. I find it a welcome friend taken daily as a preventative during 'the 'flu season' as well as a great boon to recovery if you feel yourself coming down with an infection.

Perfect Calmer

There is one more herb which can be enormously helpful especially when you become so wound up that you find it difficult to come down or to do any form of meditation or relaxation. That herb is valerian. Long used as a fragrance in perfume and soap, as a seasoning in soups and salads, and as a sedative for relieving anxiety, insomnia and chronic pain, valerian – *Valeriana officinalis* – lives up beautifully to its folk reputation as a natural tranquilliser. Recent research confirms that this common herb, which blooms with tiny rose-coloured flowers from June to September, has a remarkable ability to normalize the workings of the central nervous system. Like a few of the finest herbs, it appears to act as a sedative in states of agitation yet as a stimulant when given to counteract extreme fatigue. New studies show that valerian can lower elevated blood pressure, relax stomach muscles (and in doing so improve digestion), and even that it has natural antibiotic activity. In Germany it is commonly used to treat hyperactivity and certain behavioural problems in children. Most important of all, scientific research confirms that valerian is a superb natural sedative. In a double-blind study of 128 people performed under strict laboratory conditions, a water-based extract of valerian was given to investigate the herb's effects on sleep. One of the major problems with drug-based sleeping pills such as the barbiturates or the benzodiazepines is that while they will put you to sleep they also have negative side effects such as interfering with the quality of the sleep you get when taking them and leaving you with a 'hangover' of fatigue in the morning. Researchers found that valerian significantly improved sleep quality and decreased 'sleep latency' – the time it takes you to go to sleep – as efficiently as the drugs do. It also left subjects with no hangover the next morning and reduced night-time awakenings in insomnia sufferers. And it also works as a de-tenser. I find it particularly good when I have been travelling across time zones as a help in re-adjusting my sleep pattern. Get acquainted with a few of the best herbal stress-helpers. They are good friends to have around when you need them.

Day Nine

Sleep Deep

We are nearing the end of the *10 Day De-stress Plan* and it is about time we took a look at how well – or badly – you sleep.

Sleep is a great healer for stress. It regenerates your body, clears emotional conflicts, and helps you think and work at peak efficiency. That is as long as you get enough of it. A lot of people don't. In Britain alone 50 million sleeping pills are swallowed each year which means that for every person addicted to narcotics there are twelve hooked on barbiturates. Learn to set the stage for blissful sleep and you will go a long way towards becoming stress-wise.

Much about sleep remains a mystery in spite of the elaborate research that has been done into how and why we sleep and dream. And most of the common notions about sleep are untrue. For instance, sleep is not some kind of 'little death' from which you are rescued every morning. Nor do you go to bed to fall deeper and deeper into sleep until you reach the bottom somewhere after midnight, after which you come closer and closer to consciousness until you finally awaken. Also, deep sleep is not any more beneficial than light sleep. And we do not necessarily need the obligatory eight hours a night to remain stress-wise and well.

Two Faces of Sleep

There are two kinds of sleep: *orthodox* sleep, which is dreamless (sometimes called synchronized slow-wave sleep because of the brain-wave patterns that accompany it) and *paradoxical* sleep, during which dreaming occurs along with rapid eye movement (REM) – sometimes called desynchronized sleep. Orthodox sleep is vital for physical restoration of the body while paradoxical sleep is essential to your mental and emotional stability. Research into sleep measured by electroencephalograms has shown that all of us spend our sleep time moving in and out of these two stages in predictable rhythmic patterns. If for any reason these patterns are repeatedly disturbed, we suffer.

There are four levels or depths to orthodox sleep. When you fall asleep you move into the first level, characterized by low-amplitude fast-frequency brain-wave patterns. Sometimes sleep starts with a sudden twitching movement called a myoclonic jerk. This is the result of a sudden flare-up of electrical activity in the brain, as in a minor epileptic seizure. Then, as you move to level two and even deeper into levels three and four, there is a general slowing of the frequency and an increase in the amplitude of your brain waves. Normally you fall asleep and remain for a short time at level one and two and then plunge into levels three or four to stay there for 70 to 100 minutes. At that point comes your first period of REM or paradoxical sleep when dreams begin. This dream period of REM lasts only 10 to 20 minutes. It is repeated again at about 90-minute intervals throughout the night with orthodox, undreaming sleep in between, culminating in the longest period of REM – usually about half an hour – just before you wake up.

During orthodox sleep your body is quiet, heartbeat slows, blood pressure falls slightly, and your breathing gets slower and more regular. Even your digestive system winds down. In the deeper levels of orthodox sleep, brain waves gradually become more synchronized, as if everything is at peace. At such times your body's restorative processes come into their own, rapidly repairing damaged tissues and cells, producing antibodies to fight infection, and carrying out a myriad of other duties necessary to keep you healthy. Without orthodox sleep in all its different stages, this important vegetative restoration does not take place properly and you become more prone to stress-damage, illness, early ageing, fatigue and muddled thinking. Orthodox sleep is the master restorer.

Pure Contradiction

REM sleep, which is diametrically opposite to orthodox sleep in many ways, is just as vital. It more than earns its name 'paradoxical' by being a mass of contradictions: although the body is virtually paralysed during the REM state, the fingers and face often twitch and the genitals become erect. Breathing speeds up to the level of your normal waking state. Heartbeat rate, blood pressure and temperature rise, and adrenalin shoots through the system. Beneath the lids your eyes move rapidly from side to side as though you were looking at a film or tennis match. And this is exactly what is happening – you are viewing images that come rapidly in succession. Your brain waves in the REM state show a marked similarity to the rapid, irregular patterns of being awake.

Although the exact purpose of REM sleep remains a mystery, researchers know that it is essential for maintaining one's mental and emotional equilibrium. The need for paradoxical sleep also varies from one person to another. How much you will need is related both to your personality and your general psychological state. Longer and more frequent periods of REM sleep take place in times of psychic pain or when your defence patterns are being challenged by new demands. Women tend to have increased REM sleep during the three or four days before the beginning of a period. For most women this is a time of increased anxiety, irritability, mood changes and unstable defence patterns. But there is a lot that is not known about the function of paradoxical sleep. Well-known French researcher Michel Jouvet, who has done extensive studies of the REM state in animals and their unborn young (where it also occurs), believes it is a kind of practice of the genetic code in which the lower animals run through their instinctive behaviour patterns. In mammals and man, he thinks, it is a time when we are probably practising our learned behaviour as each night we go through the process of integrating new information with the knowledge we already have.

Psychic Necessity

When humans are deprived of REM sleep they become increasingly excitable, their appetites soar, a perverted sexuality appears, and eventually they suffer a nervous breakdown. Studies also show that even too little REM sleep makes them more restless and anxious. Their short-term memory starts to fail and they suffer from poor concentration and other unpleasant symptoms. Sleep researchers have discovered this by watching carefully and, each time subjects enter the paradoxical stage of sleep (indicated by rapid eye movements clearly visible beneath closed eye lids), they awaken them.

This aspect of REM sleep is particularly interesting, for when scientists disturb sleepers in the orthodox state, they find that deprivation of orthodox sleep doesn't lead to any psychological disturbances. But after being deprived of REM sleep for several days, sleepers become desperate for it. Their normal sleep patterns alter so that they slip into REM immediately on falling asleep and then experience 20 to 30 periods of it each night instead of the usual three. Psychologists refer to this phenomenon as 'REM rebound'. It is often accompanied by fierce nightmares as psychic imagery, too long repressed, seeks strongly to reassert itself.

Sleeping pills repress this REM phase, and repression can result in lasting psychological damage to the pill popper. After taking sleep-inducing drugs regularly, coming off them may make you fear that you are going crazy as you start to experience the REM rebound. There are other reasons to steer clear of sleep-inducing drugs. Both barbiturates and non-barbiturates prescribed for sleep are physically and psychologically addictive – barbiturates to an even greater degree than heroin. They can be fatal when mixed with alcohol in the bloodstream. Finally – something that few people realize – they are not very effective in the long-term. Sleeping pills can be successfully used to bring on sleep only for the first week or two. After that, dangerously increased doses are needed to make them work. For many people who rely on sleeping pills, the power of suggestion brought about by putting one in the mouth and swallowing it is far more useful than the drug itself in introducing sleep. And the drug itself can only do you harm in the long run, sleeping pills themselves put your body under continual stress. There are safer and more effective ways of getting to sleep.

How Much Sleep?

The amount of sleep you need varies tremendously from one person to another. It also varies from one day to the next. There is no truth in the idea that you need eight hours of sleep to stay well and feel energetic. You might need ten hours, while another person gets on very well with four and a half hours. One study showed that short sleepers tend to be active, outgoing people who are sociable, flexible in their personalities and more conformist socially. Those wanting longer periods of sleep are more introverted and creative and are particularly good at sustained work. Often the more stress-filled your day, the more sleep you will need to balance it.

As we get older we tend to sleep less. Many 60- and 70-year-olds get by on a mere three or four hours a day. Occasionally you meet someone who sleeps as little as half an hour to an hour each night, yet appears to be perfectly normal. The amount of sleep you need depends so much on your biological and psychological individuality that you can't make hard and fast rules about it. Many high achievers and great minds throughout history – Napoleon, Freud and Thomas Edison, for instance – have been poor sleepers while others like Einstein could sleep the day away. But the idea that you need a certain amount of sleep each night to stay well is a powerful one. For many people it is so embedded in their unconscious that if they only get seven hours one night instead of eight, they are convinced they will be tired the next day and soon develop all the signs of it. If you are one of these people, try re-examining the premise and experiment – sleep less and see what happens. You may find that how you feel after a certain amount of sleep depends more on your own choice than on the time spent in bed. Try sleeping less for a few days. Many people find when they do, they actually have *more* energy.

Forget Insomnia

A lot of so-called insomnia is nothing more than the result of worrying about getting to sleep. Many people who consider themselves insomniacs are really victims of the general propaganda about sleep rather than true non-sleepers. And many people seek treatment because they can only sleep four or five hours a night, although that may be all they need. There is nothing more likely to cause sleeplessness than the worry that you won't be able to drop off. Sometimes sleeplessness can be normal. After all, we all experience a sleepless night now and then, particularly if we are over-tired, worried or excited about some coming event.

Real, chronic insomnia is less frequent. A major research project into long-term insomnia turned up some interesting facts about sufferers. Over 85 per cent of the 300 insomniacs studied had one or more major pathological personality indications, such as depression, obsessive compulsive tendencies, schizophrenic characteristics or sociopathy. For them, their insomnia was a secondary symptom of a more basic conflict. Insomnia was a socially acceptable problem they could talk about without fear of being judged harshly. Insomnia is often little more than a mask for whatever is really bothering the non-sleeper. Occasionally the inability to sleep can be a manifestation of a nutritional problem – often a deficiency of zinc coupled with an excess of copper, which produces a mind that is intellectually over-active and won't wind down, or a deficiency of calcium or magnesium or vitamin E, which can lead to tension and cramping in the muscles and a difficulty in letting go.

The more easy-going an attitude you take to sleep, the less likely you are to have any problem with it. If you miss an hour or two, or if you are not sleepy, simply stay up, read a book, or finish some work. Believe it or not, one of the best times for coming up with creative ideas is in the middle of a sleepless night. It can be the perfect opportunity for turning stress into something creative. Chances are that you'll more than make up for it in the next couple of days – provided you don't get anxious about it.

How – and How Not – to Get Sleep

Next time you are troubled by sleeplessness take a look at nature's sleep aids.

• Get more exercise regularly during the day. This helps burn up stress-caused adrenalin build-up in the brain, which can result in that tense, nervous feeling where you are 'up' and can't seem to get 'down'. Don't take strenuous exercise just before going to bed as it can set the heart pounding and stimulate the whole body too much.

• Don't go to bed when you are not sleepy. Instead, pursue some pleasant activity, preferably passive. Television is not the best choice, for rays emitted from the set disturb your nervous system when you least need it.

• Don't drink coffee, alcohol or strong stimulants at dinner. This isn't just an old wives' tale. One researcher looking into the effects of caffeine on human beings recently showed that total sleep time is decreased by two hours and the mean total of intervening wakefulness more than doubles when patients are given the caffeine equivalent of a couple of cups of coffee. Alcohol may put you to sleep but it tends not to keep you there, awakening you instead in the early hours of the morning.

● Try some passiflora. Passion flower is one of the world's best natural tranquillizers. It is readily available in the form of tablets which you can take before bed or when you need a 'downer' and it is not habit-forming as are tranquillizers.

● Drink milk. It is an old-fashioned remedy, maybe, but it is scientifically sound that drinking a glass of milk before bed helps you to sleep. Milk contains tryptophan, a precursor to one of the calming brain chemicals called serotonin which is important for relaxation and for inducing sleep. High in calcium, it is often referred to as the slumber mineral because it induces muscle relaxation.

● Use an ionizer. This is a little contraption put beside your bed that sends negative ions into the air and is a godsend to anyone who has the kind of nervous system that tends to go 'up' and doesn't want to come 'down'. Although not cheap, it is an excellent investment for you can use it at a desk when you have a lot of work to do. Or, if you buy one of the portable varieties, you can also take it in the car on long trips to keep from going to sleep (it magically works both ways) and on flights to minimize the effects of jet lag. Negative ions also stimulate the production of serotonin in the brain.

● Take a lukewarm bath, submerging yourself as much as possible for ten minutes. Then, wrapping a towel around you just long enough to get rid of the drips, pop into bed immediately. Lukewarm water is the most relaxing of all temperatures on the body. A hot bath before bed is a mistake. It is far too stimulating to the heart and gets your motor running.

● Get into a rut. Go to bed as far as possible at the same time every night and develop a routine or simple ritual about it. Doing the same thing every night before going to bed quickly accustoms the mind to accept sleep.

● Write your troubles away. If you have trouble with a racing mind, rather than try to block all your thoughts, face them. Take a pen and some paper and write down all the things that come into your mind. Don't worry if you jump from one thought to another, just keep jotting down thoughts, ideas and worries. When you run out of things to write, assure yourself that you can let go of all those concerns for the night because they will be right there on the paper when you wake up.

● An excellent hydrotherapy technique for sleepless-ness is the sitz bath treatment. Fill a bath or large basin with about 13 cm (5 in) of cold water. Make sure you are warm to begin with. Lower your bottom into the bath – leaving your feet and legs hanging over the edge. Stay sitting for 30 to 45 seconds, then get out and dry yourself. Wrap up warm and go to bed.

● Another hydrotherapy technique is to take a pair of cotton socks and soak them with cold water. Wring them out well and put them on your feet. Cover the socks with a second pair of dry ones – either wool or cotton – and retire for the night.

● Listen to mellow music. Music can help alter consciousness and have you sinking blissfully into the depths of slumber. A Walkman with a few tapes by the side of your bed is one of the most pleasant ways of putting a racing mind to rest and easing yourself into sleep.

● Some of the essential plant oils have a wonderful calming effect on the mind and body. You can take a warm bath with them or place a few drops on your pillow to inhale through the night. For the bath use four drops of lavender oil, two drops of camomile and two drops of neroli (orange blossom). Or try a drop or two of each on your pillow.

● Begin each day with 20 minutes in the sun or in very bright light. Your circadian rhythms are linked to sunlight. The sun sets our natural clocks properly and acts as a natural energizer too.

● Learn to breathe deeply. It is amazingly tranquillizing and the best possible antidote to anxiety. Try this simple exercise. Lie on your bed on your back with legs drawn up, knees bent and feet flat against the bed and no pillow under your head. Place one hand on your abdomen, the other on your chest. Then, breathing in through your nose quietly and deeply, see that both hands rise with your inhalation and fall with the out-breaths *through your mouth.* Be sure to let all your breath out. There is almost always a bit more to come and most of us breathe by sticking out our chests and sucking in our tummies – all wrong! Breathe deeply but gently like this for five minutes each night before turning out your light.

● Prastise a relaxation or meditation technique (see Day Four) twice a day. A valuable tool for sleeplessness, it will lower elevated blood pressure and help you cope better with whatever stress you tend to carry off to bed with you.

● Tranquillity teas can help. Get to know the natural tranquillizers and herb teas, and whenever you feel the

138

need use them, sweetened with honey if you like, as a bedtime drink. Peppermint, camomile, skullcap, catnip and vervain are renowned for their relaxing effects.

Stop worrying about getting to sleep. Just let it happen. If it doesn't tonight, so what? It will tomorrow night. Or the next. Lack of sleep is not going to kill you, but worrying about it for long enough just might.

Go Free

Save the best until last, the old saying goes. I don't necessarily say that what comes on the tenth day of the *10 Day
De-stress Plan* is the best but in many ways it is the deepest.
For today we look at a technique that can not only
enhance your ability to deal with stress right now but it
can also help to clear away stresses that have been locked
deep within the body and the psyche for the whole of a
lifetime.

Meet Seedpower

Each one of us is utterly unique. Like the seed of a plant
that has encoded within its genetic material the characteristics that will in time produce a full-grown flower,
each of us comes into the world carrying a package of as
yet unrealized but incredibly rich potential. I call this
seedpower. This physical, psychic and spiritual potential
creates each person's uniqueness. You are rather like
the individual brushstroke a Zen painter uses to represent
one leaf on a shaft of bamboo. The leaf he paints is
totally singular, like no leaf which has ever existed, yet
within its uniqueness is encompassed universal beauty

and life energy of the highest order. So it is with each human being.

Within the individual genetic package which is you is nestled your very own brand of seedpower – an inner core that encompasses far greater physical, creative and spiritual potential than any of us could hope to realize in one lifetime. More often than not, however, the physical, emotional, spiritual and social environment in which we grow up does not support the full unfolding of our seed-power. Then, like a plant trying to develop in depleted soil with too little rain and too little sun, or a seedling trying to negotiate its way around a stone in the soil, we develop our own brand of stress and distortion.

For every situation, every experience, all thoughts, perceptions and fears that block the full expression of an individual's seedpower are stressors. These stress experiences become encoded within your body as layer upon layer of old stress and manifest themselves as muscle tension, metabolic processes that don't function as well as they should, negative thought patterns and recurring emotions such as fear, anxiety or depression. When we carry around a lot of old stress we gradually develop a lack of trust in ourselves or a lack of confidence, a feeling of being unworthy or guilty – and even a sense of mean-inglessness which can lead to an addiction or greed for material things which no matter how many you acquire never fills up the emptiness. That is where autogenics can help.

Autogenic training is a thorough and highly successful technique for relaxation, de-stressing at the very deepest levels, and personal transformation. It was developed in the early 1930s by the German psychiatrist Johannes H. Schultz. It consists of a series of simple mental exercises designed to turn off the 'fight or flight' mechanism in the body and turn on the restorative rhythm associated with

141

profound psychophysical relaxation. In doing so, layer by layer, it gently and gradually clears away stress that you have been carrying around for many years. It is a method which, when practised daily, brings results which can be comparable to those achieved by serious Eastern meditators, yet it is particularly appealing to the Western mind. For unlike many forms of meditation and yoga, autogenics has no cultural, religious or cosmological overtones and requires no special clothing or unusual postures or practices. But perhaps most appealing, as the name implies, is that what happens when you practise is generated from *within*. A person using autogenic training has no external values or philosophies imposed upon him or her. It is the perfect tool for stress release and freeing seedpower from the inside out.

Freedom to Be

Schultz was a student of the clinically orientated neuropathologist Oskar Vogt who, at the turn of the century at the Berlin Neurological Institute, was deeply involved in research on sleep and hypnosis. Vogt remarked that some of his patients who had been subjected to conventional forms of hypnosis soon developed the ability to put themselves in and out of a hypnotic state – or rather autohypnotic, since it was self-induced. He noticed that these patients experienced remarkable relief from tension and fatigue and also tended to lose whatever psychosomatic disorders they had been suffering from. Schultz drew on Vogt's observations and went on to design techniques for individuals to be able to induce this deep mental and psychological relaxation at will.

Schultz noticed that people entering the autohypnotic state experience two specific physical phenomena: the first was a sensation of heaviness in their limbs and torso, and the second a feeling of diffuse warmth throughout the body. The warmth is the result of vasodilation in the peripheral arteries and the sensation of heaviness is caused by deep relaxation in the body's muscles. Schultz figured that if he taught people to suggest to themselves these things were happening to their bodies he could rapidly and simply introduce them to the state of what he called *passive concentration* which characterizes the auto-hypnotic state and which exercises great positive influence over the autonomic nervous system to restore imbalances from prolonged stress.

Until then the autonomic nervous system had been considered beyond the realm of conscious control. Remember the autonomic nervous system's two branches – the sympathetic and the parasympathetic? They are more or less opposite in their actions and together they govern bodily functions and reactions such as gastric secretions, the flow of adrenalin, the arousal that goes with the fight or flight stress reaction, constriction and dilatation of blood vessels, heart rate, breathing and lots of other bodily changes which we cannot consciously control. The sympathetic branch, if you remember, is concerned with arousal – the active dynamic state asso-ciated with stress and necessary for movement and for accomplishment in life. The parasympathetic is concerned with psychophysical relaxation, recuperation and the proper functioning of the body's internal organs. Of course the two branches are designed to work in perfect balance and the secret of making stress work for you rather than against you is simply being able to move at will from a sympathetic-dominated state to a parasym-pathetic-dominated one and back again.

Lift Off

Most people tend to get stuck in the sympathetic-dominated stressed state: gradually symptoms of anxiety,
depression, insomnia and strain appear, and sometimes
more serious stress-related conditions such as coronary
heart disease, high blood pressure, ulcers, migraine and
exhaustion. Schultz found that his patients soon developed a capacity to switch from the sympathetic- to the
parasympathetic-dominated state so that they no longer
remained trapped. Indeed the simple practice he had
developed went even further than that. The patients not
only found themselves able to deal with current stress
levels easily in a way that was difficult to describe, they
began to eliminate 'old' stress which had accumulated in
the body over the years in rather the same way the body
eliminates physical wastes when put on a detoxification
diet. As old stress lifted off, in its place came improved
mental and bodily functioning plus the elimination of
maladaptive behaviour, together with whatever neurotic
or psychosomatic symptoms accompanied it. It was quite
a discovery. The German scientific community found it
hard to believe something so simple could have such a
profound effect.

The early mind researchers had discovered that in a
state of passive concentration all the activities governed
by the autonomic nervous system can indeed be influ-
enced by the person himself – not by his exercising any
conscious act of *will* but rather by learning to abandon
himself to an ongoing organismic process. This strange
paradox of self-induced passivity is central to the workings
of autogenic training. It also closely parallels the so-called
passive volition of biofeedback training and meditation.
It is a skill which Eastern yogis, famous for their ability to
resist cold and heat, to change the rate of their heartbeat,

levitate and perform many other extraordinary feats, have long practised. Until the development of biofeedback and autogenic training and the arrival of Eastern meditation techniques, this passive concentration largely remained a curiosity in the West, where active, logical, linear, verbal thinking is encouraged to the detriment of the innate ability to simply *experience*. In fact, many psychologists and physicians working in the field of stress studies and stress control believe that it is over-emphasis on the use of the conscious will in the West that makes us so prone to stress-based illnesses in the first place.

Heaviness and Warmth

To help his patients induce the autogenic state, Schultz worked first with the sensations of heaviness and warmth. He then added suggestions about regularity of heartbeat and gentle quiet breathing (two more natural physiological characteristics of relaxation) and went on to the sensation of abdominal warmth and coolness in the forehead. These six physiologically orientated directions – heaviness and warmth in the legs and arms, regulation of the heartbeat and breathing, abdominal warmth and cooling of the forehead – became the core of autogenic training and are known as the Autogenic Standard Exercises. A person learning autogenic training goes through each of the six steps, one by one, each time he practises. Because of the body and mind's ability with repetition to slip more and more rapidly into the deeply relaxed yet highly aware autogenic state, the formula becomes increasingly shortened until, after a few weeks or months of practising, a state of profound psychophysical relaxation can be induced at will. And, once the exercises have been mastered, they can be practised anywhere – even sitting on a bus.

A key principle on which autogenics is based is that the body will naturally balance itself when allowed to enter a relaxed state. The benefits of being able to do this are innumerable, some of them instant. Patients with high blood pressure have experienced drops in systolic blood pressure of from 11 to 25 per cent and more, as well as 5 to 15 per cent in diastolic pressure. Brain-wave activity changes so that there is a better balance of right and left hemisphere, leading to improved creativity at work and in relationships and a better sense of being at peace with oneself. Recoveries from bronchial asthma and a whole range of other psychosomatic disorders have been reported, as well as the highly successful modification of self-destructive behaviour patterns and habits such as drug-taking, compulsive eating and alcoholism. As a result autogenic training is now given as a standard treatment.

Be Here Now

There are two important aspects to making autogenic training work for you. The first is a real *acceptance* of your current circumstances or position – that is anything that you feel, whatever it happens to be. When doing autogenic training you accept that certain things for the moment cannot be changed. You simply let them be for the time being – right now. For it is only through acceptance that we open the gateways to change. The second important thing about autogenic training is self-discipline. You need to make time to do the exercises each day and to establish a routine – especially for the first four weeks during which the exercises need to be done three times a day. It takes about five or ten minutes at a time to run through autogenic training while you are learning it. The exercises can be done much more quickly once you have learned them. Rather like Pavlov's dog (who learned to salivate at the sound of the bell because the bell sounded and the food appeared together over and over again), the way that autogenic training begins to work on your body depends on the continual repetition of its use again and again, day after day. Once the initial period of learning is completed, you can then use the exercises once or twice a day or whenever you like and you will have gained a life-long skill that is invaluable.

The basic exercises are simple. Taking up one of three optional postures – sitting slumped rather like a rag doll on a stool, lounging in an easy chair, or lying on your back with your arms at your side – make sure you are reasonably protected from noise and disturbances and that your clothes are loose and comfortable. Generally speaking it is easiest to learn lying flat on a floor or on a very firm bed. Then once you have got the exercise under your belt, you can do it sitting up or even very discreetly on the bus on the way to work. If you like, you can record the autogenic exercise on tape and play it to yourself in the beginning, although I generally find it better to learn it very simply from the words given in the box. Here's how.

Lie down on your back in bed and make yourself comfortable. Close your eyes gently. Take a deep slow breath and pause for a moment. Now exhale fully and completely. Allow yourself to breathe slowly and naturally. Feel your body sinking back into the floor. Then repeat the following phrases to yourself slowly and allow yourself to feel the heaviness and warmth as you do.

The first phrase is: 'My left arm is heavy… my left arm is heavy… my left arm is heavy… my right arm is heavy… my right arm is heavy… my right arm is heavy…' Allow yourself to let go of any tension in your arms as you say to yourself: 'My left arm is heavy… my left arm is heavy… my left arm is heavy…', repeating each suggestion three times.

Continue to breathe slowly and naturally, remembering to exhale fully. Say to yourself: 'Both arms are heavy… both arms are heavy… both arms are heavy.' Let go of any tension in your arms. Then say: 'Both legs are heavy… both legs are heavy… both legs are heavy…'

As you continue to breathe slowly and naturally, say to yourself: 'Arms and legs heavy… arms and legs heavy… arms and legs heavy… arms and legs warm… arms and legs warm… arms and legs warm…' Feel the warmth flow through to your arms and legs as you say to yourself: 'Arms and legs warm… arms and legs warm… arms and legs warm…'

Continue to breathe slowly and freely while you repeat silently to yourself: 'My breathing calm and easy… my breathing calm and easy… my breathing calm and easy… my heartbeat calm and easy… my heartbeat calm and easy… my heartbeat calm and easy…' Feel your strong, regular heartbeat as you say these words to yourself.

Continue to breathe easily and say to yourself: 'My solar plexus is warm… my solar plexus is warm… my solar plexus is warm…' Feel the muscles in your face relax as you say to yourself: 'My forehead is cool and clear… my forehead is cool and clear… my forehead is cool and clear…'

Enjoy the feeling of softness and calm throughout your body and say to yourself: 'I am at peace… I am at peace… I am at peace…'

When you have finished the exercise you are ready for the return that will bring you back to normal everyday consciousness. Quickly clench both fists, take a deep breath in, flex both arms up in a stretch, then breathe out slowly and completely, returning your arms with unclenched fists to your sides. Open your eyes. Lie for a moment with your eyes open and just allow yourself to

BE HERE NOW WITH WHATEVER IS.

When practising autogenics, each suggestion is repeated three times and the entire exercise itself needs to be repeated at three different periods each day. The best time is generally just before you get out of bed, just before you go to sleep and at some time during the day. If there is no possibility of lying down during the day to repeat the exercise you can always do it sitting up in a chair. If you are in public draw your fists up to your chest by bending your elbows rather than bringing the whole arm above the head. Before long even the simple suggestion 'my left arm is heavy' will trigger the psychophysical relaxation process in the whole body. Some people get feelings of heaviness and warmth immediately, for others it takes as long as a week or two of practising three times a day for 10 or 15 minutes at a time. But for everyone it comes eventually and with it comes a profound sense of relaxation.

Autogenic Training Made Simple

With both eyes closed repeat the following suggestions, each one three times:

- MY LEFT ARM IS HEAVY... MY RIGHT ARM IS HEAVY
- BOTH ARMS ARE HEAVY... BOTH LEGS ARE HEAVY
- ARMS AND LEGS HEAVY... ARMS AND LEGS WARM
- BREATHING CALM AND EASY... MY HEARTBEAT CALM AND EASY
- MY SOLAR PLEXUS IS WARM... MY FOREHEAD IS COOL
- I AM AT PEACE

The return

- CLENCH BOTH FISTS
- TAKE A DEEP BREATH
- FLEX BOTH ARMS UP IN A STRETCH
- BREATHE OUT SLOWLY
- RETURN ARMS
- UNCLENCH FISTS

Mind Mystery

Just why such a simple mental exercise should bring about such profound benefits is at least a partial mystery. The neurophysiological mechanism by which the autonomic nervous system is controlled is by no means completely understood.

One of the most common questions asked about autogenic training is how does it differ from various Eastern meditative techniques such as transcendental meditation and Zen? Although autogenic training brings about a similar 'low-arousal' state, where parasympathetic activity dominates, unlike classical meditation it stems from exercises meant specifically to induce simple *physical* sensations leading to a state of relaxation of a purely physical nature. Yet the experiences which accompany its practice are fascinating: in addition to slowing the heartbeat, reducing blood pressure and improving depth of respiration, changes in the reticular activating system in the brain stem can bring about what are known as 'autogenic discharges' – a spontaneous way of 'de-stressing' the body and eliminating old tensions. Autogenic discharges can manifest themselves as temporary twitching of the arms or legs – much like the twitch experienced occasionally on falling into a deep sleep – during the session itself, or increased peristaltic movement (stomach grumbles) or various transient feelings of dizziness or visual or auditory effects. These phenomena are harmless, quick to come and go yet, say autogenic practitioners, an important part of throwing out life-accumulated, stressful material stored in the body.

A few people (including myself), when they first begin autogenic training, go through two or three weeks where a lot of ancient stress gets released through autogenic discharge while old feelings of discouragement or depression rise to the surface. It is important to be aware of this possibility and to know that it is little more than stored stress rising to the surface in order to be eliminated. Because of this discharge phenomenon, some psychologists in the English-speaking world who teach autogenics like to work on a one-to-one basis with their students in order to help them gain perspective on what is coming up from their consciousness. In Germany this is not considered important. There, autogenic training is taught as a matter of course both to adults and school children with no such psychological back-up. The important thing to remember is that whatever happens to rise to the surface is likely to be very old indeed – stress you have been carrying around for a long time and which you are far better off without. Within four to six weeks of autogenics most people begin to experience a steady and increasing release of creative energy, and a sense that great burdens are being lifted away, so that – often for the first time – they begin to feel free to live their own life.

Born Free

Re-balancing your body and reclaiming energy that has been locked up in long-term stress demands that you go to your core. It is at your core that true freedom is to be found. The process of rediscovering freedom is a gradual one which entails letting go of distorted habit patterns, fears and frustrations which you may have developed, and reasserting trust in yourself.

Go back now and look at the list of stressors you made on Day One. How do they seem now? Have any shifted columns? Has your perspective on any of them altered as a result of changes in your diet or taking up relaxation or thanks to new insights? It is a good idea to carry out this same exercise again every month or so. You are likely to find that many subtle but pervasive shifts take place in your ways of handling stress and even in your values.

In most of us, detoxification – a real clear-out – needs to take place on a psychological and spiritual level as well as a physical one. We tend to carry around a load of false ideas, notions and habit patterns, which either suppress or squander our core energy, making us highly susceptible to stress-damage. They need gradually to be dissolved or thrown off. They are false because they are not authentic to ourselves – they have not grown spontaneously out of our own brand of seedpower. Such rubbish, in its own way, can be as big an energy-drainer as living on junk food.

I hope that some of the information, exercises, tools and techniques in this book which have helped many others, including myself, will also be of use to you in clearing away what does not rightly belong to you or doesn't serve you. But do remember that all of what is in this book is here for one purpose only – to serve *you*. *You* are not here to serve *it*. What works for you, make use of. What does not, discard. There is no perfect path to becoming stress-wise. Each of us is here to cut our own path and, in doing so, to express as fully as possible our own individual nature. That is where real freedom lies. Such freedom is not only the key to becoming stress-hardy, it is a never-ending source of joy and creativity. Go for it!

Resources

These are my favourite outlets. To find your local suppliers, contact your nearest health-food shop and they can provide details.

Autogenic training: To work with a trained practitioner contact the Centre for Positive Health, 101 Harley Street, London W1. Tel: 071 935 1811.

Dandelion coffee: My favourite coffee substitute is dandelion coffee, the sort that you grind like coffee beans and use in the same way in a filter coffee maker or cafetière. For your nearest stockists contact Cotswold Health Works Ltd, 5–6 Tabernacle Road, Watton Under Edge, Gloucestershire GL12 7EF. Tel: 0453 843 694.

Essential oils: I particularly like essential oils from Gerard and from Tisserand. For a list of essential oils contact Gerard, Natural Image Ltd, Ashby House, Bath Street, Ashby de la Zouch, Leicestershire LE65 1NZ. Tel: 0530 563900. For Tisserand products contact Tisserand Aromatherapy Products, Knoll Business Centre, Old Shoreham Road, Hove, Sussex BN3 7GS. Tel: 0273 412 139.

Frownband: This is an ingenious little device that helps 'de-stress' the face. Made of nylon, a frownband is worn like a headband which not only takes unconscious tension out of the forehead but actually erases many of the lines that have been etched into it by frowning. For further information contact Julia Hastings, PO Box 47, Haslemere, Surrey GU27 2RW.

Herbs: Valerian & suma are available from Solgar (see p.155). The best form of echinacea is called Echinaforce from Bioforce, who also do a passiflora product, Passiflora Incarnata. For stockists contact Bioforce UK Ltd, Olympic Business Park, Dundonald, Ayrshire KA2 9BE. Tel: 0563 851177. For stockists of Siberian ginseng contact R.H. & M. Victuals Ltd, Gardiner House, Broomhill Road, Wandsworth, London SW18 4JQ. The best ginseng comes in the form of Jinlin Ginseng Tea – available from health-food stores. If you have difficulty finding it, contact Alice Chiu, 4 Tring Close, Barkingside, Essex IG2 7LQ. Tel: 081 550 9900; Fax: 081 551 8100.

Honey: The Garvin Honey Company have a good selection of set and clear honeys from all over the world. These can be ordered from The Garvin Honey Company Ltd, Garvin House, 158 Twickenham Road, Isleworth, Middlesex TW7 7DL. Tel: 081 560 7171. The New Zealand Natural Food Company have a good range of honey, in particular Manuka honey, known for its anti-bacterial effects. The New Zealand Natural Food Company Ltd, 9 Holt Close, Highgate Wood, London N10 3HW. Tel: 081 444 5660.

Juice extractor: Moulinex do an inexpensive centrifugal juicer which is good.

Marigold Swiss vegetable bouillon: This instant broth powder based on vegetables and sea salt is available from health-food stores or direct from Marigold Foods, Unit 10, St Pancras Commercial Centre, 63 Pratt Street, London NW1 0BY. Tel: 071 267 7368. It comes in regular and low-salt forms. The low-salt form is excellent for making spirulina broth.

Nutritional supplements: Solgar do excellent multiple vitamins and minerals – my favourite being their VM2000. For stockists contact Solgar Vitamins Ltd, PO Box 398, Chesham, Bucks HP5 3EY. Tel: 0494 791 691. For lower potency supplements with high bio-availability, Nature's Own do unique vitamins which, through a patented process, have been bonded to food proteins to render them highly bio-available and assimilable. Their minerals are put through a biotec process that organically ties them to a food matrix. They do an excellent Vitamin B-complex, good niacin, beta-carotene, calcium and magnesium, as well as other single vitamins and minerals. For shops nearest you contact Nature's Own, 203–205 West Malvern Road, West Malvern, Worcs WR14 4BB. Tel: 0684 892 555; Fax: 0684 892 643.

Sea plants: Nori and red, green and brown algae can be bought from Japanese grocers or macrobiotic health shops.

Super greens: Spirulina, alfalfa, barley and carrot/barley/spirulina powders are available by mail order from Xynergy Products, Ash House, Stedham, Midhurst, West Sussex GU29 0PT. Tel: 0730 813642. Chlorella is available in capsule form from Solgar Vitamins Ltd, PO Box 398, Chesham, Bucks HP5 3EY. Tel: 0494 791 691.

Index

Page numbers in **bold** type refer to major discussions

acetylcholines 16
adaptive energy 13-14, 116
adaptogens, 116, **118-23**
addiction, to exercise **80-1**
adenosine triphosphate (ATP) 78
adrenal glands 111
adrenalin 11, 13, 15, 16, 77-8, 130
adrenalin build-up **77-8**, 135
aerobic exercise 25
agar-agar 35
alarm stage 13
alcohol 19-20, 38, 69, 79, 80, 97,
    132, 135-6, 146
alfalfa 30, 31, **33-4**
algae **31-3**, **34-5**, 35
alginates 97
alkalinity 32
amino acids 31, 32, 95
anaemia 32
anti-oxidants 33
anxiety 26, 79, 94, 144
Apple Slaw 41
arteriosclerosis 91, 92, 93, 95, 96
arthritis 91, 96
asthma 56, 146
autogenics **141-51**
autonomic nervous system **16-18**,
    68, 143, 150
auxones 29
awareness, passive **67-8**, 108-9
Ayurvedic medicine 106

back, relaxation position 46-7
backache 55, 61
barbiturates 127, 128, 132
barley, green 30, 31, **34**

baths 136, 137
Benson, Herbert 69, **72-4**, 108
beta-carotene 33
biofeedback 144-5
bioflavonoids 33, 103
biotin 103
Bircher-Benner, Max 29-30
Bircher Muesli 40
blood-sugar levels 39
blue-green algae 31
bodymind **105-6**, **111-13**
boron 103
brain:
    adrenalin build-up 77-8, 135
    autogenics 150
    brain waves 67-8, 109, 129, 130,
        146
    development **107-8**
    effects of fatty diet 91
    exercise and 77-8, 80
    left-brain worldview **106-7**
    relaxation response **108-9**
    right brain **109-10**
    serotonin and 96, 136
    sleep 129, 130
breakfast 36
breathing 45, 47-8, 71-2, 138
Brekhman, I.I. 119, 121, 122, 123

cabbage, Apple Slaw 41
caffeine 19-20, 39, **93-4**, 135
calcium 33, 95, 103, 134, 136
callisthenics 76
caloric energy 13
calories 97, 98
camomile tea 38
cancer 96
carbohydrates 90, **92-3**, **95-6**, 97-8
The Cat, intrinsic yoga **61-4**

156

catecholamines 16, 124
cells 27, 28, 30, 78, 91
centre of stillness **66-7**
CGF (Chlorella Growth Factor) 34
Chad 32
challenges, attitudes to 25
chlorella 30, 31, **34-5**
chlorophyll 34
cholesterol 90
choline 103
chromium 95, 97, 103
cigarette smoking 19-20, 69, 80-1
Cobra, intrinsic yoga **55-7**
coffee 38, 39, **93-4**, 97, 135
colon 49
comfrey tea 38
commitment 25
constipation 49
control, lack of 25-6
copper 33, 103, 134
corticoid hormones 11, 124
cortisone 18
Country Salad 42
creativity 112-13, 135
Crocodile, intrinsic yoga **52-4**, **57-9**
Curetin, Professor Tom 79

dairy products 100
de Vries, Herbert 79
delegation 23
depression 26, 79, 80, 94, 144
detoxifying body **27-42**
diabetes 90, 93, 96
diet **90-104**
  alfalfa **33-4**
  barley **34**
  carbohydrates **95-6**
  chlorella **34-5**
  coffee **93-4**
  detoxifying body **27-42**
  fats **90-2**
  green foods **30-6**
  hunger 25
  processed food 35, 90
  protein **94-5**
  raw food **28-30**, 36, 96
  recipes **40-2**
  seaweeds **35**, **97**
  spirulina **31-3**
  stress-wise **97-102**

stressors 19-20
sugar **92-3**
vitamin and mineral supplements
  102-4
digestive leucocytosis 29
digestive system 28-30, 49
dinner 37
discipline **70-1**
disease, resistance to 18
DNA 34, 124
dreams 129
dried fruit, Yoghurt Energy Blend
  40-1
drinks 37-9, 101
  coffee 38, 39, **93-4**, 97, 135
  Green Drink 42
  herbal teas 38, 138-9
  spring-clean diet 37-9
  stress-wise diet 101
  stressors 19-20
  tea 38, 93
drugs 69, 79, 146
  sleeping pills 127, 128, 132
  tranquillizers 79, 116, 136, 138-9
dulse 97

eating habits 27
  see also diet
ecdysone 124
ECG stress tests 84-5
echinacea 116, **124-6**
eleuthrococcus senticosus **122-3**
emotional stress **20-1**
emotions, mood and **78-80**
employment 20-1, 23, 24-5
energy:
  adaptive 13-14, 116
  exercise and **77-8**, **87**
  total involvement and **88-9**
enzymes 30, 31, 33
Eppinger, Professor 30
essential fatty acids 91
exercise 19, 25, **75-89**, 135
exhaustion stage 13, 14

fatigue, coffee drinking and 39
fats, in diet 19-20, **90-2**, 97-8, 100
fibre 93, 96, 97
fight or flight mechanism **15-16**,
  77, 141-2

fish 100
Flamingo, intrinsic yoga **48-50**
folic acid 103
food *see* diet
fruit 25, 28, 91, 95-6, 98, 101
fruit juices 38, 39
frustration 43

gastric ulcers 94
General Adaptation Syndrome
  (GAS) 12-13, 14
ginseng **119-23**
Glasser, William 80
golden rod tea 38
gout 90
grains 99
Green Drink 42
green foods **30-6**
Greist, John 79

Half-Scissor, intrinsic yoga **60-1**
'hara' centre 87
headaches 39, 55
heart, adrenalin build-up 77-8
heart disease 82, 84-5, 93, 144
heavy metals 34, 35
helplessness 26
herb teas 38
herbs **116-27**
here and now 87, **88-9**
hero image 23
high blood pressure 17, 45, 84,
  114, 144, 146
high-energy people 14, 88-9
homeostasis 12, 27
homotoxins 124
hormones:
  acetylcholines 16
  adrenalin 11, 13, 15, 16, 77-8,
    130, 135
  catecholamines 16
  corticoid 11, 18, 124
  exercise and 79-80
  fight or flight mechanism 15, 16
  noradrenalin 79-80
  psychoneuroimmunology 111
hunger 25
hydrotherapy 137
hypertension 17
hypnosis **142-3**

hypoglycaemia 39
hypothalamus 111

imagination **113-14**
immune system 18, 34, 124, **125-6**
inactivity 19
'inner voice' 66
inositol 103
insomnia 80, **126-7**, **134-5**, 144
instinctive self 43
insulin 39, 92
intellect 43, **106-7**, 108
interferon 34
intrinsic yoga **43-65**
iodine 97, 103
ionizers 136
iron 32, 33, 95, 103

jogging 86
*Journal of the American Medical
  Association* 12
Jouvet, Michel 131

kelp 35, 97
kombu 35, 97
Krishnamurti 73

lactates 18, 68
Lazarev, N.V. 119
lemon grass tea 38
lemon verbena tea 38
leucocytosis, digestive 29
lime blossom tea 38
lithium 97
lunch 37
lungs 47

magnesium 33, 95, 103, 134
manganese 33, 103
mantras, meditation 73
Mason, Marilyn 44, 45, 65
maximum mind 108-9
meat 94-5, 100
meditation **69-74**, 83, **108-9**, 113,
  138, 142, 150
menopause 33
menus 36-8, **99, 102**
metabolism 18, 27, 30, 32
methionine 33
migraine 55, 114, 144

milk 136
mind 43, **105-15**
minerals 28, 30, 31, 95, 97, **102-4**
mitochondria 78
molybdenum 103
mood, exercise and **78-80**
Morgan, William P. 79
Muesli, Bircher 40
Murphy, Michael 83-4
music 137

natural rhythms 14
neck:
  relaxation position 47
  tension 55
negative ions 136
nervous system 13, **16-18**, 68, 77,
  126, 143, 150
neuropeptides 111
noradrenalin (norepinephrine)
  79-80
nori 97
Nut/Seed Mix 40

oestrogen 33
oils 91, 100
osteoporosis 95
oxygen 18, 31, 68, 80, 91

PABA 103
pancreas 39, 92
pantothenic acid 33
parasympathetic nervous system
  16-18, 68, 143, 144
passiflora (passion flower) 38, 136,
  139
passive awareness **67-8**, 108-9
peppermint tea 38
personal growth **81-3**
personality types 81-2
physical inactivity 19
pituitary gland 111
plant oils 138
posture 54
potassium 33, 103
Pottenger, Dr. S.M. 29
pre-menstrual tension 33
priorities 24
processed food 35, 90
protein 32, 33, **94-5**, 97-8

psychoneuroimmunology (PNI)
  111-12
pulse, taking 88
pulses, in diet 94-5, 100

Rainbow, intrinsic yoga **50-1**
raw food **28-30**, 36, 96
reasoning self 43
rebounding 86
recipes **40-2**
red algae 35
relaxation **67-74**, **108-9**
  autogenics **141-51**
  creativity and 112-13
  discipline **70**
  effects on body 18, **68-70**
  passive awareness **67-8**
  relaxation position **46-8**
  'relaxation response' 69, **72-4**,
    108-9, 110
  and sleep 138
  yoga 45
  zazen **71-2**
religion 83-4
REM sleep **129-32**
repetition, meditation 108
requests, giving in to 23
resistance stage 13
respiratory system 56
RNA 34
routine 24

salads 41-2
  Apple Slaw 41
  Country Salad 42
saturated fats 91
Schultz, Johannes H. 141-5
sciatica 60
seaweeds **35**, **97**
sedatives **126-7**
seedpower **140-2**
seeds, Nut/Seed Mix 40
selenium 33, 103
self-esteem **81-3**
Selye, Hans 9-10, 11, 14, 116, 119
serotonin 96, 136
Shaw, George Bernard 44
Sheehan, Dr George 76-7
Shoulder Bridge, intrinsic yoga
  51-2

shoulders, relaxation position 47
Siberian Ginseng **122-3**
sitz baths 137
sleep 67, 80, **126-7, 128-39**
sleeping pills 127, 128, 132
smoking 19-20, 69, 80-1
soft drinks 38
solidago tea 38
Solomon, Dr G.F. 111
spine 45, 54, 55, 60
spirulina 30, **31-3**
spring-clean diet **27-42**
spring water 38
stamina 80
stress:
  definition **11-12**
  listing stressors **21-2**
  reaction to **12-13**
  relaxation and **68-70**
  stress-hardy people **25-6**
  unnecessary **19**
stress-wise diet **97-102**
subconscious self 43
sugar 19-20, **92-3**
suma **123-4**
sunlight 138
superconscious 111
superfoods 30-1
superhuman syndrome 21, 23
swimming 86
sympathetic nervous system 13,
  16-18, 77, 143, 144

tea 38, 93
  herbal 38, 138-9
television 135
tension 47, 54
thrush 125
time management 23-4
tobacco 19-20
total involvement **88-9**
toxins **27-42**
tranquillizers 79, 116, 136, 138-9
Transcendental Meditation **69-70**,
  150
tryptophan 136

unconscious mind **109-10**, 111,
  114-15
unnecessary stress **19**

unsaturated fats 91
Unsupported Cobra, intrinsic yoga
  54-7
uric acid 90-1

valerian 116, 118, **126-7**
values 23
vanadium 97
vegetable juices 38, 39
vegetables 28, 41, 91, 94-5, 98, 101
vitamins 28, 30, **102-4**
  vitamin A 33, 103
  vitamin B complex 33, 35, 92,
    103
  vitamin B1 33, 103
  vitamin B2 103
  vitamin B3 103
  vitamin B5 33, 103
  vitamin B6 33, 103
  vitamin B12 32, 33, 103
  vitamin C 33, 103
  vitamin D 33, 103
  vitamin E 33, 103, 134
  vitamin K 33
Vogt, Oskar 142

walking 79, **85-7**
water 38
wheat grass 31
White, Rhea A. 83-4
white blood cells 29-30
willpower 78
winding down from work **24-5**
work 20-1, 23, 24-5
worldview **105-6**, 107, 112

yoga **43-65**
  The Cat **61-4**
  Crocodile **52-4, 57-9**
  Flamingo **48-50**
  Half-Scissor **60-1**
  Rainbow **50-1**
  relaxation position **46-8**
  Shoulder Bridge **51-2**
  Unsupported Cobra **54-7**
Yoghurt Energy Blend 40-1

zazen **71-2**
Zen Buddhism 84, 150
zinc 33, 95, 103, 134